AT THE NUCLEAR CROSSROADS

Choices about Nuclear Weapons and Extension of the Non-Proliferation Treaty

Edited by
John B. Rhinelander
and
Adam M. Scheinman

University Press of America, Inc.
Lanham • New York • London

The Lawyers Alliance for World Security

Lawyers Alliance for World Security
Committee for National Security
Washington Council on Non-Proliferation

All three entities are co-located and cooperate on a series of projects focusing on the interrelationship of U.S. national security policy and American non-proliferation objectives. Cooperative activities include Field Visits by senior national security experts to local communities around the United States, Washington-based luncheon briefings on nuclear, chemical and biological weapons control issues, and research, publication and distribution of Issue Briefs and other works on critical weapons proliferation issues. A partial list of principals involved in the three entities include Paul C. Warnke, Robert S. McNamara, William E. Colby, Lawrence J. Korb, Adam Yarmolinsky, John B. Rhinelander, James F. Leonard, and George Bunn. A list of publications appears at the end of this volume.

LAWS gratefully acknowledges the support of the Carnegie Corporation of New York, the John Merck Fund and the W. Alton Jones Foundation. The views expressed in this volume are solely those of the authors.

ISBN 0–8191–9817–X (cloth : alk. paper)
ISBN 0–8191–9818–8 (pbk. : alk. paper)

Dedicated to the memory of
Ambassador Gerard C. Smith,
nuclear arms control
pioneer & practitioner

Table of Contents

PREFACE

No issue has so gripped the U.S. defense and arms control communities than the threat of nuclear proliferation. Public exposure to this concern is reinforced almost daily in news and other media coverage of U.S. and other efforts to confront North Korea's nuclear-bomb ambitions, to defuse a potential nuclear flare-up in South Asia, or to staunch the flow of nuclear contraband from the former Soviet Union. The American public recognizes in these threats clear risks to U.S security. What receives far less exposure in the media, and is thus less apparent to the general public, is the inherently unstable balance between U.S. efforts to prevent others from acquiring or even using nuclear weapons, while the U.S. itself continues to rely on nuclear weapons for security. To quote General Charles Horner, the outgoing chief of the U.S. Space Command, "It's kind of hard for us to say to North Korea, 'You're terrible people, you're developing a nuclear weapon,' when we have 8,000."

The chapters in this volume all reflect the fundamental inter-action between the choices the United States makes on its nuclear weapons policy on the one hand, and its broader nuclear non-proliferation goals on the other. Fostering public understanding and education of arms control and non-proliferation issues and concerns is a principal aim of the Lawyers Alliance for World Security (LAWS), a Washington-based non-governmental organization, which in association with the Committee for National Security and the Washington Council on Non-Proliferation, previously published some or all of the chapters contained here. These organizations share an interest in seeing the Non-Proliferation Treaty extended for the longest possible term in 1995, but recognize that such an event can only be assured if the United States and the other acknowledged nuclear-weapon states are seen to be sincerely trying to reduce and ultimately eliminate their nuclear-weapon holdings.

At the Nuclear Crossroads

LAWS wishes to express its gratitude for the generous support it has received from the W. Alton Jones Foundation, the Carnegie Corporation of New York and the John Merck Fund. LAWS would also like to thank Chris Behan for helping to prepare these articles in a single volume.

Philip A. Fleming, Esq.
President, LAWS

John V. Parachini
Executive Director, LAWS

Washington, DC
October 1994

About the Authors

GEORGE BUNN is Member-in-Residence of the Stanford University Center for International Security and Arms Control. He has been an attorney for the U.S. Atomic Energy and Nuclear Regulatory Commissions, a member of a Washington law firm, and a professor and dean at the University of Wisconsin Law School. He was General Counsel of the U.S. Arms Control and Disarmament Agency and a member of the U.S. delegation that negotiated the NPT during the 1960s, becoming a U.S. Ambassador to the Geneva Disarmament Conference in 1968.

DAVID A. KOPLOW is a Professor of Law at the Georgetown University Law Center in Washington, D.C., where he teaches courses in public international law and a seminar on the "Proliferation of Modern Weapons." He is the author of numerous articles on arms control and international law topics, including studies of treaty obligations, U.S. constitutional law and verification. From 1977-1980, he was an Attorney-Advisor in the Office of the General Counsel at the U.S. Arms Control and Disarmament Agency, and a Special Assistant to the Director of the Agency. He is the Vice-Chair of the Lawyers Alliance for World Security.

JAMES F. LEONARD is President of the Washington Council on Non-Proliferation. A retired career foreign service officer, he held positions as Assistant Director of the U.S. Arms Control and Disarmament Agency, U.S. Ambassador to the Geneva Disarmament Conference, Deputy Chief of Mission, U.S. Mission to the UN, and Deputy Special Negotiator to the Middle East Peace Negotiations. He has also served as President of the United Nations Association and as Advisor to the Palme Commission.

JOHN B. RHINELANDER is a senior partner in the law firm of Shaw, Pittman, Potts & Trowbridge and an adjunct professor at Georgetown University. He is Vice Chairman of the Board of Directors of the Arms Control Association and a member of the Board of the Lawyers Alliance for World Security. He is a former Legal Advisor at the Department of State and former Legal Advisor to the U.S. SALT I Delegation. Mr. Rhinelander also held the positions as General Counsel at the Department of Health, Education and Welfare and UnderSecretary of the Department of Housing and Urban Development.

ADAM M. SCHEINMAN is Senior Policy Analyst for Arms Control and Non-Proliferation with the Lawyers Alliance for World Security. From 1990 through 1993, he was Program Coordinator and Research Analyst for the Washington Council on Non-Proliferation. He has also worked with both the Foreign Affairs and National Defense and Environmental and Natural Resources Policy Divisions of the Congressional Research Service, Library of Congress. Mr. Scheinman received his M.A. in 1990 from George Washington University and his B.A. in 1987 from Cornell University.

ROLAND M. TIMERBAEV is Visiting Professor and Ambassador-in-Residence at the Monterey Institute of International Studies. Before retiring from the Russian Foreign Ministry, he had a 40-year career as a diplomat. During that career, he participated in most of the important arms control negotiations involving the Soviet Union, including the Non-Proliferation Treaty and the Comprehensive Test Ban. He was most recently Russia's Permanent Representative to the International Atomic Energy Agency. He is co-director of a project at the Monterey Institute of International Studies on the role of international organizations in non-proliferation.

CHARLES N. VAN DOREN is a Principal Consultant in the international division of Ogden Environmental and Energy Services Company, Fairfax, Virginia. Mr. Van Doren served as Assistant Director of the U.S. Arms Control and Disarmament Agency from 1977-1981, heading its Non-Proliferation Bureau. Throughout his 19-year career at ACDA, which included 8 years as Deputy General Counsel, Mr. Van Doren specialized in non-proliferation and nuclear export matters. He participated in the negotiation of the NPT and in all subsequent phases of its implementation, including service as Alternate U.S. representative to the 1975 and 1980 NPT Review Conferences.

FIGURE 1. World Nuclear Testing in the Last Seven Years: 1988–1994

"The negotiation of a comprehensive and verifiable ban on nuclear explosions . . . reflects our common desire to take decisive action that will support and supplement the global nuclear non-proliferation regime and will further constrain the acquisition and development of nuclear weapons . . . ."

— President Bill Clinton

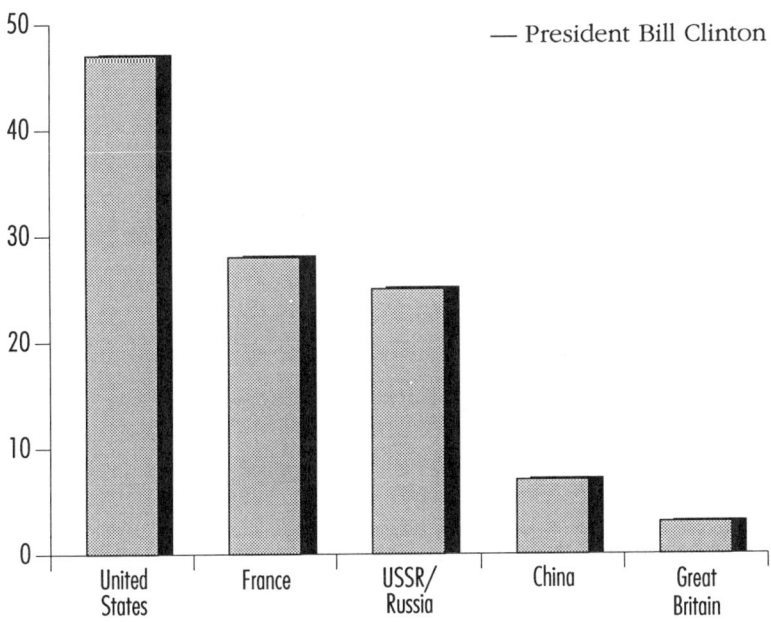

Sources: Arms Control Association, Natural Resources Defense Council

FIGURE 2. Performance of the Nuclear Powers

Despite recent astonishing achievements in nuclear arms control, U.S. and Russian land- and sea-based long-range forces after START II, and total British, French and Chinese nuclear forces, will exceed 1970 levels when the NPT entered into force.

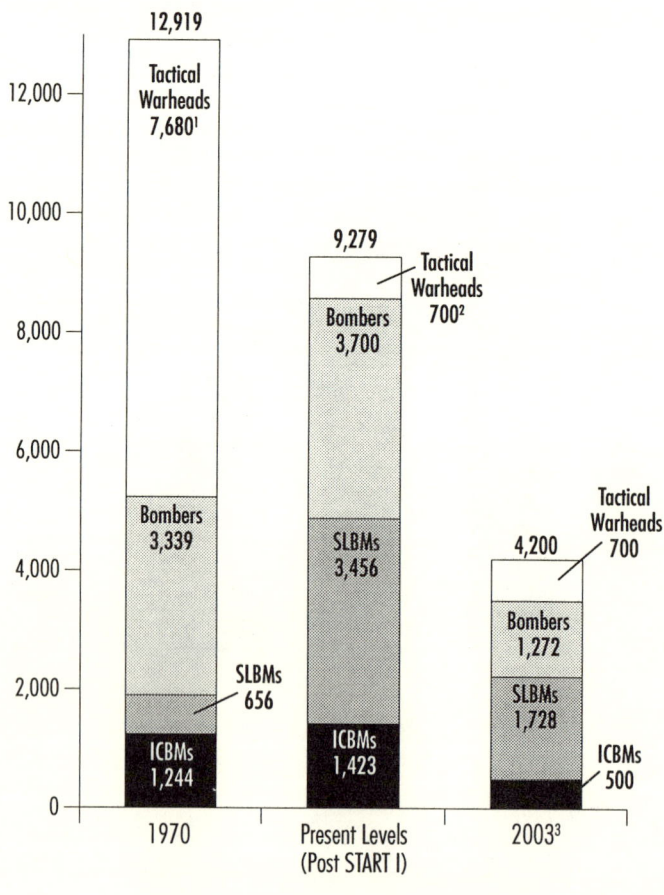

U.S. Deployed/Active Nuclear Forces

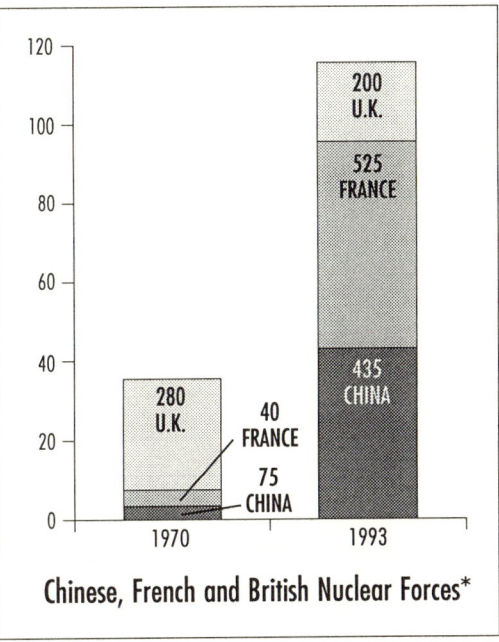

Graph by Daniel Knott and Adam Scheinman.

Sources: *The Bomb Book: The Nuclear Arms Race in Facts and Figures,* Dec. 1987; *The Bulletin of the Atomic Scientists,* Dec. 1993; *Arms Control Today,* April 1991, July 1992, and Dec. 1992; *NATO's Theater Nuclear Force Modernization Program: The Real Issues,* Jeffrey Record, Nov. 1981; "U.S. Decides to Withdraw A-Weapons from S. Korea," Don Oberdorfer, The Washington Post, Oct. 20, 1991; *SIPRI Yearbook 1992: World Armaments and Disarmament; SIPRI Yearbook 1993: World Armaments and Disarmament; The Military Balance: 1970–1971.*

Chinese, French and British Nuclear Forces*

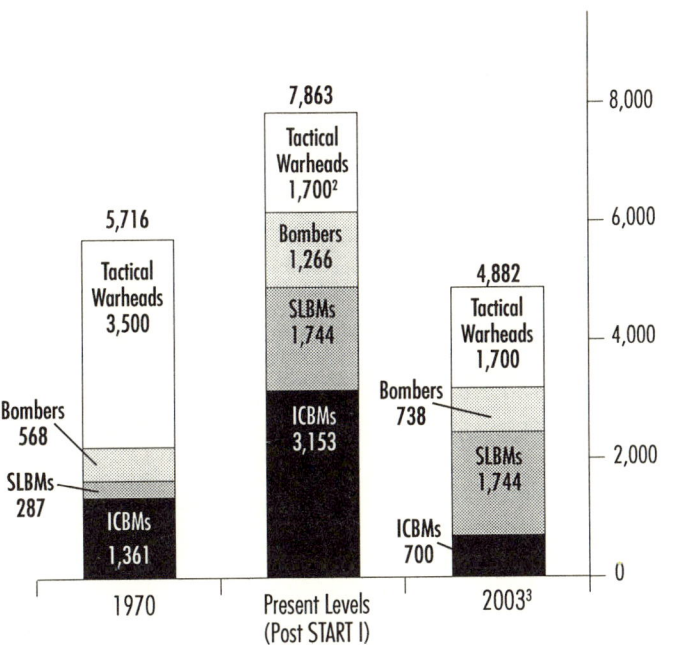

Notes:

* Indicates total warheads in the stockpile.

1 Estimated NATO forces and U.S. tactical nuclear deployments in South Korea.

2 Estimated tactical nuclear deployments after 1991–92 Bush/ Gorbachev/Yeltsin unilateral cutbacks.

3 Projected forces after START II and assuming constant levels of tactical deployments.

Soviet/Russian Deployed/Active Nuclear Forces

FIGURE 3. Knocking on the Nuclear Door

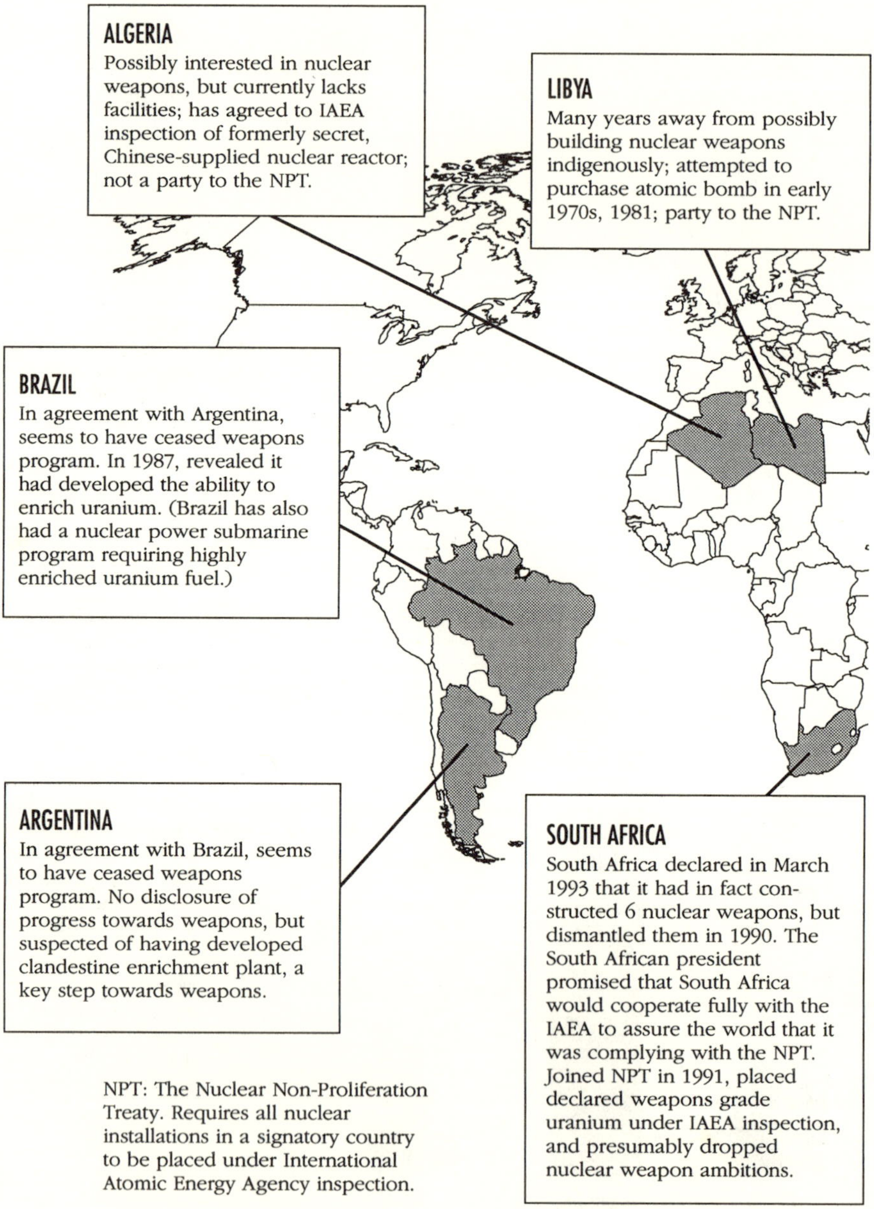

ALGERIA
Possibly interested in nuclear weapons, but currently lacks facilities; has agreed to IAEA inspection of formerly secret, Chinese-supplied nuclear reactor; not a party to the NPT.

LIBYA
Many years away from possibly building nuclear weapons indigenously; attempted to purchase atomic bomb in early 1970s, 1981; party to the NPT.

BRAZIL
In agreement with Argentina, seems to have ceased weapons program. In 1987, revealed it had developed the ability to enrich uranium. (Brazil has also had a nuclear power submarine program requiring highly enriched uranium fuel.)

ARGENTINA
In agreement with Brazil, seems to have ceased weapons program. No disclosure of progress towards weapons, but suspected of having developed clandestine enrichment plant, a key step towards weapons.

SOUTH AFRICA
South Africa declared in March 1993 that it had in fact constructed 6 nuclear weapons, but dismantled them in 1990. The South African president promised that South Africa would cooperate fully with the IAEA to assure the world that it was complying with the NPT. Joined NPT in 1991, placed declared weapons grade uranium under IAEA inspection, and presumably dropped nuclear weapon ambitions.

NPT: The Nuclear Non-Proliferation Treaty. Requires all nuclear installations in a signatory country to be placed under International Atomic Energy Agency inspection.

Sources: Leonard S. Spector with Jacqueline R. Smith, Nuclear Ambitions, (Westview Press, 1990), p.6; Office of Technology Assessment, Proliferation of Weapons of Mass Destruction: Assessing the Risks (Washington, DC, August 1993), p. 64.

PAKISTAN
Undoubtedly has nuclear weapon program, probably successful. U.S. President no longer certifies to Congress that Pakistan does not possess a nuclear device, suggesting high likelihood that it does.

INDIA
Exploded a nuclear device in 1974; probably has sufficient materials for several weapons.

NORTH KOREA
Suspicious reactor and reprocessing laboratory; submitted to some some IAEA inspections in 1992 and 1993, but refused others; in March 1993, denied IAEA access to suspected reprocessing waste sites and declared its intention to withdraw from NPT (since rescinded).

TAIWAN
Has sizeable nuclear power program, but lacks facilities to produce materials for nuclear weapons; built secret lab to extract plutonium in 1987, but dismantled unit under U.S. pressure before plutonium obtained (made similar attempt in mid-1970s, also thwarted by U.S.); party to NPT.

IRAQ
Massive program uncovered after Gulf War; United Nations has required destruction of most infrastructure, but knowledgeable personnel still in country.

IRAN
Reportedly pursuing nuclear weapons, but little public evidence of progress; CIA testimony estimated production unlikely before the end of the decade without foreign assistance.

ISRAEL
Widely believed to have a clandestine nuclear arsenal of approximately 100 weapons.

Editors' Introduction

John B. Rhinelander and
Adam M. Scheinman

In 1995, the more than 160 parties states to the 1968 Non-Proliferation Treaty (NPT) will have an opportunity to meet at the United Nations headquarters in New York City in what could be the most important arms control summit of the century—the NPT Extension Conference. An extension decision in favor of unlimited duration would help preserve the impressive gains in non-proliferation and arms control that have followed the end of the Cold War, and set the stage for even greater progress in the future. Conversely, a short or limited extension decision would brake the momentum on arms control and introduce uncertainty, and could encourage some defense planners in both nuclear and non-nuclear states to reserve all military options, including nuclear ones. In this scenario, the NPT and associated arms control agreements and initiatives will have ceased to operate as an effective barrier to proliferation, and would be difficult if not impossible to replace. Given the stakes involved, ensuring the NPT's long-term survival as an enduring norm is a first-order priority.

According to Article X.2 of the treaty, the extension decision, which is to be approved by a simple majority vote of all the parties, can be taken in one of three ways: indefinite extension, extension for a single fixed period, or extension for additional fixed periods. The U.S. supports the indefinite continuation of the NPT in recognition of the treaty's central role in global efforts to prevent nuclear proliferation. However, given the wide range of interests, motivations and perceptions that states will carry with them to the conference, the optimum outcome—indefinite extension—may be the most difficult to achieve, although that is not an argument for dropping it. The U.S. and its indefinite extension "allies," which includes among others the nations of the Conference on Security and Cooperation in Europe, the G-7 and the South Pacific Forum, do not provide the more than 80 votes necessary for a majority decision. The nations of the Non-Aligned Movement (NAM) form the largest NPT voting block, numbering more than 100, and winning the support of many of them is a *sine qua non* for success in 1995.

Two factors typically reflected in the current statements of leading NAM nations work against indefinite extension. The first applies to the treaty's fundamental discrimination between the five nuclear "haves" and the "have nots." The non-nuclear-weapon states (NNWS) are concerned that a vote for indefinite extension of the treaty would sanction the nuclear powers' (the United States, Russia, the United Kingdom, France and China) right to hold onto their nuclear arsenals indefinitely into the future. As described in *Nuclear Disarmament: How Much Have the Five Nuclear Powers Promised in the Non-Proliferation Treaty* by George Bunn and Roland Timerbaev (two principal negotiators of the NPT for the United States and Soviet Union respectively) and James Leonard (former United States ambassador to the Geneva Committee on Disarmament [CD]), the initial twenty-five year term of the NPT and the 1995 extension conference function as a lever for the NNWS to pressure the five nuclear-weapon parties to do more than freeze the status quo. (It also offers the opportunity for some states to pressure one or more of the three "threshold" nuclear-weapon states that have not joined the NPT, particularly Israel, to either accede to the treaty or "freeze" their nuclear programs.) This position, although justifiable, is shortsighted if coupled with a limited extension of the NPT and in the final analysis falls outside of everyone's best security interests. The NPT is the only arms control instrument in which the nuclear powers have consented to work towards nuclear disarmament, and they will only consider much deeper reductions of nuclear forces or undertake significant nuclear constraints in the context of a robust treaty that prohibits proliferation.

The second factor relates to the stated interest of some non-nuclear states in retaining a future nuclear weapons option should changes in the international system—e.g. should North Korea or a successor state to the former Soviet Union threaten its neighbors with nuclear aggression—ever require it to be exercised. Yet, under any of the three authorized extension options, parties to the NPT retain the right to withdraw if "extraordinary events, related to the subject matter of the [NPT], have jeopardized their supreme national interests." (Article X.1.) More broadly, however, American and other officials need to assert in clear terms that it is precisely because uncertainty and disorder are likely to remain prominent features of the post-Cold War international system that a strong NPT regime is needed.

However compelling these arguments may appear, states take a typically conservative approach to decisions effecting their military security, and therefore to support indefinite extension, i.e. to abjure nuclear weapons permanently while the nuclear powers retain their arsenals, will not be an easy vote to cast. If at the 1995 conference no majority for indefinite extension, or even a very narrow majority, appears likely, American negotiators may well consider next-best options. George Bunn and Charles Van Doren (a former ACDA Assistant Director for Non-Proliferation) in *Two Options for the 1995 NPT Extension Conference Revisited* analyze the "additional fixed . . . periods" option, and determine that an extension of the treaty for *an indefinite number of successive fixed periods,* e.g. twenty-five years each, wherein a majority of states parties could vote to terminate the treaty at the end of any such period, would conform with the logic and language of the treaty. Furthermore, as Bunn and Van Doren suggest, exercising this option would purchase *de facto* indefinite extension without requiring the treaty's amendment. The NPT contains an amendment procedure (Article VIII) that contains such difficult steps in practice that amendment is not a feasible option.

Beyond state-to-state contacts during the run-up to the 1995 extension conference, what can the nuclear powers do to ensure either *de jure* or *de facto* indefinite extension? Of the treaty's provisions, Article VI attracts the greatest attention of the NNWS. At the four previous NPT review conferences, which have taken place at five-year intervals beginning in 1975, differences over Article VI were prominent and the underlying issues remain unsettled. At two of those conferences, in 1980 and 1990, the insistence of a group of non-nuclear states to interpret compliance with Article VI to include the conclusion of a comprehensive test ban treaty (CTB) forced an adjournment without the issuance of a consensus Final Document. Discord over Article VI is likely to remain if not widen as 1995 approaches, with a number of key NNWS insisting on clear commitments, supported by tangible progress on nuclear arms control and doctrine, that the nuclear powers will work to end the discrimination inherent in the NPT.

During the run-up to the extension conference and at the conference itself (which will run approximately three weeks), the United States and Russia will seek to deflect potential criticism by preparing working papers detailing their compliance with Article VI. (Britain and France are also be expected to prepare such papers, noting planned reductions in their overall nuclear firepower.) To be sure, the United States and Russia have either undertaken or agreed to sweeping reductions in tactical and strategic nuclear weapons to meet today's post-strategic deterrence international environment. This includes (1) the withdrawal or destruction of all ground- and sea-based tactical missiles from Europe, Eurasia, and Korea (in the case of the U.S.), (2) reduction of NATO's air-based nuclear deterrent by half, and (3) U.S.-Russian agreement to go down to 3,000–3,500 deployed strategic warheads after implementation of the START I and II treaties early next century. These reductions, coupled with the 1987 INF Treaty, which eliminated an entire class of intermediate-range (500–5,500 kilometers) U.S. and Soviet nuclear missiles, as well as U.S.-Russian declarations to reduce the alert status of their active nuclear forces and U.S.-Russian, British-Russian and Russian-Chinese agreements not to target one another with these forces, represent real progress that goes far towards meeting their obligation under Article VI to roll back the arms race, but which may not go far enough.

As George Bunn and Roland Timerbaev discuss in depth, the language of the NPT, the treaty's negotiating history and the subsequent practice of the parties in implementing the treaty reveal that the nuclear powers agreed to do much more when they signed the treaty. Article VI of the treaty calls on all parties to pursue negotiations in "good faith" on measures to halt the arms race and to work towards nuclear disarmament. Bunn and Timerbaev, as well as Professor David Koplow in *Nuclear Testing and the Non-Proliferation*

Treaty inform us that in August 1968 the United States, Soviet Union and the United Kingdom (France and China did not join the NPT until 1991 and 1992, respectively, although they did so without reservation and are therefore bound by the terms of Article VI) and the 15 other members of the Geneva disarmament conference gave meaning to Article VI by agreeing to take up an agenda of arms control measures under Article VI, including a CTB, non-use of nuclear weapons, a cut-off of fissile material production for weapons use and "the reduction and subsequent elimination of nuclear stockpiles . . . ."[1] The phrase "good faith" has an ambiguous quality, but as Koplow argues ambiguity is quite different from having no meaning at all. Koplow takes the argument even further by implying that until CTB negotiations resumed early this year, the U.S. had been acting in violation of Article VI.[2] Although some lawyers may not be entirely persuaded by Koplow's argument, there should be little doubt that the surest obstacle to a long-term extension of the NPT would be for the nuclear-weapon states to fail to follow through on the agenda of issues that are of the greatest concern to the non-nuclear-weapon states.

Where do nuclear negotiations stand on these concerns? To its credit, the Clinton administration has adopted a pro-active stance on a range of nuclear weapons control issues, although its follow through leaves much to be desired. On the test ban, the administration declared on March 15, 1994 that it would continue a moratorium on testing through September 1995—irrespective of whether other states test, such as China did on June 10, 1994—to boost prospects for the NPT's indefinite extension.[3] This, paired with the administration's support for the resumption of CTB negotiations in the CD, reversed 13 years of United States government antipathy to a CTB. Real progress towards a CTB has been made since negotiations resumed in early 1994, but its completion by April 1995 appears next to impossible. The greatest hindrance is the cautious attitudes and unconstructive positions of France, Britain and China on a series of substantive issues, coupled with the fact that the United States has in effect given each a veto over early progress. Without President Clinton's active involvement at the highest level to accelerate the pace of negotiations, and a decision by him to exercise effective leadership, a finished CTB treaty may not be achieved in the next year or two at the earliest—if ever.

Progress on security assurances is probably the second most important "constraint" that the nuclear powers can bring to the extension conference. Key non-nuclear states such as Nigeria and Egypt have for years called on the nuclear powers to offer binding promises not to use or threaten to use nuclear weapons against states that have foresworn nuclear weapons possession. The five nuclear states are on record in two instances in this regard. In 1968, the United States, Soviet Union (now Russia) and the U.K. promised to assist states subjected to nuclear blackmail (a so-called positive security assurance) in Security Council Resolution 255, and since 1978 the United States, Russia, Britain and France have offered unilateral assurances not to use or threaten to use nuclear weapons against states party to the NPT or similar arrangements (e.g. a nuclear-weapon-free zone), except in the case of an attack on themselves. Since joining the nuclear club in 1964, China has offered the unequivocal and unqualified assurance that it would never initiate use of nuclear weapons. Hopes that the passing of the Cold War would lead the United States to adopt—as China has—a "no first use" policy were squelched with President Clinton's decision to endorse the results of the Pentagon's Nuclear Posture Review, which, *inter alia*, retains the option to use nuclear weapons as a "last resort" against non-nuclear attacks on U.S. territory or forces.[4] The President's decision will clearly not embolden efforts by U.S. representatives to press for a permanent treaty renewal at the NPT extension conference in New York.

To address this key problem, George Bunn in *Strengthening Nuclear Non-Proliferation Security Assurances for Non-Nuclear-Weapon States* proposes that the United States and the other nuclear powers harmonize their nuclear employment doctrines in a combined positive and negative security assurance—without exceptions—promulgated through the UN Security Council, and supported by a declaration of each of the five "not to use or threaten to use nuclear weapons first against any state that is observing an international obligation not to acquire nuclear weapons . . ." Bunn's proposal goes considerably beyond what the nuclear powers are currently considering in the context of reinforcements to the non-proliferation structure. As a practical matter, a weaker assurance, which the United States, Russia and the United Kingdom have offered Ukraine once it joins the

NPT,[5] may prove to be the most that the five can coalesce around before 1995, although the non-aligned states are likely to ask for more. The non-aligneds would also undoubtedly prefer to confirm such assurances in the form of a treaty, much as their non-nuclear status is treaty bound. However, if passed through a resolution of the Security Council, the assurance—whether it is the Bunn model or another variant—the assurance would have the virtue of binding all five nuclear powers, thus helping to assuage the concerns of non-aligned and other NNWS, although each of the five could veto specific Security Council actions at a later date.

Some progress is also apparent in the area of a fissile material cut-off. The United States and Russia have agreed to support a global cut-off treaty, and towards that end, the United States, which announced a unilateral halt in fissile material production in 1992, is helping Russia to phase out and ultimately end plutonium production at its remaining plants by the year 2000. In addition, the negotiation of a cut-off treaty was referred in January 1994 to the CD, which tasked the Canadian ambassador to that body with surveying views on such a treaty's reach and negotiating mandate. The results of the survey confirmed what most states, nuclear and non-nuclear, already suspected—that differences over treaty scope, verification and the special problems created by the civil plutonium programs of Japan, France and several others preclude early agreement on a negotiating mandate for a treaty.

On "nuclear reductions and the subsequent elimination of nuclear stockpiles," there are some limited steps to commend. While the dramatic reductions of United States and Russia nuclear forces covered by START I are taking place even before the treaty is ratified (it will not enter into force until Ukraine joins the NPT, which it may soon do), neither START I nor START II deal with the fissile materials removed from deactivated systems. In addition, Britain, France and China have yet to be brought into the reductions process, and will in all probability elect to remain outside of such discussions at least until the United States and Russia agree to deeper cuts in their nuclear arsenals—perhaps to a level of 1,000–1,500 strategic warheads. To preempt inevitable criticism focused on Article VI at the extension conference, James Leonard suggests in an annex to the Bunn and Timerbaev chapter that the United States lead efforts to convene a Five-Plus-One negotiating forum, reflecting the necessity of involving all five nuclear-weapon states as well as an international monitor in these nuclear discussions. The mandate for these talks might include safety and transparency of nuclear stockpiles, as well as the acceptance by the United States and Russia of an intermediate force-level goal of 1,000–1,500 nuclear weapons in exchange for a commitment by the other three to cap their arsenals at 500 weapons. Such a forum could also provide a useful venue for advancing a program for moving to zero nuclear weapons, recognizing the certainty that elimination may be years if not decades away. If approved by the UN General Assembly before the opening of the extension conference, the mandate would establish a strong basis for sustaining the type of world envisioned in the preamble and articles of the NPT.

Much of the nuclear-weapons establishment in the United States and other nuclear-weapon states will not sympathize with Leonard's proposed Five-Plus-One negotiation. Some will reject it outright as illusory and out of step with international realities, much as the Pentagon's Nuclear Posture Review does by rejecting negotiated or unilateral reductions of United States strategic forces to force levels substantially below START II (3,000–3,500), and by retaining 500 air-based tactical nuclear weapons in Europe, mainly for symbolic reasons.[6] The attitude reflected in the Pentagon's Nuclear Posture Review in fact reflects a deep divide over the direction of American security policy in response to the threat of proliferation of weapons of mass destruction in the post-Cold War world. To some, the end of bipolarity will inevitably lead more rather than fewer states to acquire nuclear weapons for their security. Some, the argument goes, will be Saddam Hussein-like tyrants, irresponsible and irrational leaders who might use small nuclear arsenals to further their regional or geostrategic ambitions.[7] This camp is typically suspicious of "traditional" non-proliferation tools, such as diplomacy, verification safeguards and even the utility of the NPT itself. Some envision battlefield roles for nuclear weapons in regional settings, particularly in light of a perceived increase in a biological warfare threat.

Recognizing that serious and even intractable proliferation problems remain, others admonish that the vast majority of states are still strongly anti-nuclear and hostile to any proliferation. The firm international response to proliferation in Iraq and North Korea is illustrative of the international community's determination to confront proliferant nations. Further, regime enhancements in the areas of International Atomic Energy Agency safeguards, multilateral export controls and international sanctions against non-proliferation violators give greater force to the NPT's prohibitions. Arms control advocates to non-proliferation seek to delegitimize nuclear weapons as appropriate tools of national power, except as a deterrent to use of nuclear weapons by others. As George Bunn and Wolfgang Panofsky suggest in a recent issue of *Arms Control Today*, "the five declared nuclear-weapon states must demonstrate through their conduct and nuclear doctrines that they are not seeking further benefits from the possession of nuclear weapons. *In nuclear matters, self-restraint is self-interest.*"[8] To the extent the Clinton administration's ambiguously conceived "counterproliferation" initiative and the Nuclear Posture Review contemplate roles for nuclear forces beyond the deterrence of the use of nuclear weapons by others, the gains in arms control that the U.S. and the other four nuclear powers seek from the 1995 NPT extension conference will be undermined, as will be the treaty itself.

1.
Nuclear Disarmament
How Much Have the Five Nuclear Powers Promised in the Non-Proliferation Treaty?

George Bunn and Roland M. Timerbaev

Introduction

The 1968 Nuclear Non-Proliferation Treaty (NPT) constitutes a bargain between five nuclear-weapon powers (Britain, China, France, Russia and the United States) and 160 other NPT parties that do not have nuclear weapons (See Appendix B for a listing of NPT parties states). The non-nuclear-weapon parties, among other things, agree not to acquire nuclear weapons without insisting that the five give up their weapons—at least for the time being. Instead, under Article VI of the NPT, all parties agree "to pursue negotiations in good faith on effective measures relating to cessation of the nuclear arms race at an early date and to nuclear disarmament, and on a treaty on general and complete disarmament under strict and effective international control."[1] (See Appendix A for a full text of the treaty.)

The purpose of this paper is to consider the meaning of this language. Under what circumstances does Article VI obligate the five NPT nuclear-weapon parties to negotiate toward zero nuclear weapons in national arsenals? Must there *first* be agreement on more measures designed to limit the production and use of nuclear weapons, greater reductions in nuclear weapons, fewer international tensions or sharp cuts in conventional arms? Is it sufficient for the present to negotiate toward the lesser goal of Article VI, "cessation of the nuclear arms race"? (Long-sought measures toward that goal are a ban on all nuclear tests, a restraint in the production of fissionable material for nuclear weapons, and a prohibition on the use of nuclear weapons except in response to a nuclear attack.) In an attempt to answer these and related questions, we will look at the text of the NPT, its negotiating history, and the practice of its members in implementing its terms.

The negotiation of the NPT during the mid-1960s was led by the Soviet Union and the United States—then the two "co-chairs" of the multilateral Geneva disarmament conference. The treaty's main purpose was to halt the spread of nuclear weapons to additional countries beyond the five that had tested nuclear weapons by 1967— Britain, China, France, the Soviet Union and the United States.[2] It has been joined by more than 155 non-nuclear-weapon countries having the same goal. But, unwilling to legitimize forever a "discriminatory" world divided between the five that had nuclear weapons and the many that did not, those without nuclear weapons forced a compromise. The compromise limited the NPT to a first term of 25 years; imposed Article VI on the nuclear-weapon parties; required review of the NPT every five years to determine whether this and other obligations were being realized; called for such a review in the same year (1995) that the parties were to decide by majority vote how much longer the treaty should last; and established the right to withdraw from the treaty if "extraordinary events" relating to nuclear non-proliferation jeopardized "the supreme interests" of a party concerned.[3] As described below, the NPT's negotiating history and the practice of the parties in implementing it suggest that a reason for this compromise, from the point of view of the non-nuclear-weapon countries, was to keep pressure on the nuclear-weapon powers to halt the nuclear arms race and to move toward zero nuclear weapons. First, however, let us turn to Article VI itself to look for an answer to the question of *when* negotiation toward *zero* nuclear weapons is required.

The Meaning of Article VI as Derived from its Text

Article VI itself shows that first priority was to be given to negotiation of measures "relating to cessation of the nuclear arms race." This phrase was followed immediately by "at an early date." In contrast, Article VI's call for negotiations relating to "nuclear disarmament" and on "general and complete disarmament" was not qualified by language suggesting that their achievement was to be given similar urgency. Article VI clearly gave priority to "cessation-of-the-nuclear-arms-race" measures. While not stating that they had to be negotiated first—before nuclear-reductions talks became obligatory—it gave them greater urgency.

When Article VI was negotiated, both American and Soviet plans for "general and complete disarmament" on the Geneva negotiating table called for zero *national* nuclear weapons by the third and last stage of disarmament.[4] This was, however, only to be undertaken in conjunction with world-wide reductions of national armed forces and conventional arms to very low levels. In the U.S. plan, the preconditions for moving to zero included reduced international tension, improved mechanisms for peaceful settlement of international disputes, and a strengthened United Nations peace force.[5]

Did Article VI establish the same linkages and pre-conditions for "nuclear disarmament" as Soviet or U.S. plans did for "general and complete disarmament"? The Article VI obligation to negotiate on measures "*relating* to . . . nuclear disarmament" (emphasis added) could include a variety of measures that would reduce deployed nuclear weapons to levels far short of zero. Did Article VI require negotiation of "nuclear disarmament"—meaning zero national nuclear weapons—without the accompanying drastic reductions in conventional weapons and armed forces contemplated by both the American and Soviet plans for general and complete disarmament? Did the requirement include the reduction in tensions and the strengthened UN, as called for by the American plan?

"Disarmament" can sometimes mean reductions short of zero.[6] However, the ordinary meaning of "nuclear disarmament" clearly *includes* zero even if it also includes reductions short of zero. Therefore, the obligation to negotiate on measures "relating to . . . nuclear disarmament" seems to include, among other things, zero. Thus, one meaning of Article VI, probably its plainest, is for eventual negotiations dealing with the elimination of nuclear weapons through either of two routes: (1) toward "nuclear disarmament" without linkages and preconditions, and (2) toward "general and complete disarmament" with them.

The NPT's preamble, however, suggests a different meaning. It contains two relevant provisions, one suggesting the purpose of negotiations relating to "nuclear disarmament," and the other of negotiations—concurrent or sequential—relating to "general and complete disarmament." In the first provision, the parties declare:

> their intention to achieve at the earliest possible date the cessation of the nuclear arms race and to take effective measures *in the direction of* nuclear disarmament . . . . [7]

In the second instance, the parties state their desire:

> to further the easing of international tension and the strengthening of trust between States in order to facilitate the cessation of the manufacture of nuclear weapons, the liquidation of all their existing stockpiles, and the elimination from national arsenals of nuclear weapons and the means of their delivery *pursuant to a treaty* on general and complete disarmament under strict and effective international control . . . . [8]

The contrasting language of these two preambular provisions suggests that Article VI does not require negotiation on proposals calling for zero nuclear weapons except in the context of general and complete disarmament, including the pre-conditions—easing of international tensions and strengthening of trust between states. At the same time, "effective measures *in the direction of nuclear disarmament*" (but presumably short of it) are to be pursued without reference to general and complete disarmament or to such conditions precedent. Therefore, one could argue from the preamble that the achievement of complete nuclear disarmament was only contemplated in the context of general and complete disarmament.

There is thus some conflict between the plain meaning of Article VI itself and the preambular provisions suggesting its purpose. However, the negotiating history of the treaty and the practice of the parties suggest that pursuit of zero was foreseen along two alternative routes: one to "nuclear disarmament" without a requirement of linkages and pre-conditions, and the other to "general and complete disarmament" with linkages and pre-conditions.

The Meaning of Article VI as Derived from its Negotiating History

In 1962, soon after the adoption of the "Irish resolution" by the UN General Assembly calling for a non-proliferation agreement, the United States met with a group of its NATO allies who were also members of the multilateral Geneva disarmament conference where such an agreement was to be discussed. Two U.S.-proposed options considered at this meeting were declarations by countries having nuclear weapons not to disseminate them to those that did not, and separate declarations by those that did not—not to acquire them. At the meeting, Italy expressed reservations about such declarations unless there were promises from the countries having nuclear weapons to get rid of them eventually.[9] Later in 1962, the Italians acquiesced in a revised U.S. non-dissemination draft for the countries having nuclear weapons. This draft would not have required a non-acquisition promise from countries not having them, and it would have permitted the use of U.S. nuclear weapons by a multilaterally-manned naval force of NATO countries (the so-called MLF) in which Italy could participate.[10] The Soviet Union, however, rejected this draft.[11]

Criticism of a non-proliferation accord that discriminated by permitting some but not others to have nuclear weapons was thus raised originally by a U.S. ally—Italy. Moreover, the Italians seemed to speak for the Germans as well; for Cold War reasons, the Federal Republic of Germany (West Germany) had not at that point been invited to participate in the Geneva disarmament conference.[12] When the Italians later proposed that countries not having nuclear weapons forswear acquiring them in short-term unilateral declarations pending negotiation of additional obligations for those having nuclear weapons (including steps toward nuclear disarmament), German Chancellor Erhard announced that Germany had already signed a non-acquisition declaration and called upon others to follow suit.[13] This Italian-German idea seemed to imply that if they and other countries with the potential to make nuclear weapons renounced them, the nuclear-weapon powers should take steps toward nuclear disarmament.

> *The measures mentioned most often in the negotiating history are a test ban, cut-off and prohibition on use.*

When the focus later shifted to Soviet and U.S. drafts for a non-proliferation treaty of unlimited duration, Germany pointed out that more was needed than such a "limited" NPT:

> It is incumbent on the nuclear-weapon powers to stop the further development of increasingly more dangerous weapons, not to increase existing stocks, including the means of their delivery, to begin reducing them, to stop the production of fissionable material for military purposes, and to aim at a comprehensive test ban. When the nuclear-weapon powers explicitly announce their willingness to take their own steps to restrict and reduce armaments, a limited non-proliferation treaty would be the beginning of international cooperation for a genuine guarantee of peace in the nuclear age . . . . The execution of the promised disarmament measures [by nuclear-weapon powers] couldbe checked by an international authority at each further stage of disarmament process . . . . The nuclear-weapon powers are called upon to take the next steps . . . . [14]

This statement was issued after several years of negotiations had made agreement on an NPT seem possible in the near future. The first public U.S. draft NPT in 1965 had been followed soon by a Soviet counter proposal. Both called for a treaty of unlimited duration that would prohibit those having nuclear weapons from disseminating them to those that did not, and that would prohibit those that did not have nuclear weapons from acquiring them. Neither draft contained any article obligating the countries having nuclear weapons to negotiate an end to the nuclear arms race or to reduce their nuclear arsenals. The major differences concerned how they would deal with existing and planned multilateral arrangements within NATO for control over nuclear weapons that might be used in response to an attack by the Soviet-led Warsaw Pact.[15]

At Geneva, Italy submitted a draft short-term "unilateral-renunciation" declaration for advanced non-nuclear-weapon countries that was essentially a counter proposal to the draft U.S. treaty. In the Italian proposal, the non-nuclear-weapon declarants were to meet just before the end of an initial term of years to review "the progress which has been made toward international agreements to prevent the spread of nuclear weapons, or to halt the nuclear arms race, and to reduce nuclear arsenals." Any decision by these declarants to extend their declarations would be based upon this review—including, clearly, what progress the nuclear-weapon powers had made toward limiting and reducing their nuclear weapons.[16]

The "Non-Aligned Eight," the non-aligned, non-nuclear-weapon countries represented at the Geneva conference, then made the same point about a non-proliferation treaty:

> A treaty on non-proliferation of nuclear weapons is not an end in itself but only a means to an end. That end is the achievement of *general and complete disarmament, and, more particularly, nuclear disarmament.* The eight delegations are convinced that measures to prohibit the spread of nuclear weapons should, therefore, be *coupled with or followed by tangible steps,* to halt the nuclear arms race and to limit, reduce and eliminate stocks of nuclear weapons and the means of their delivery.[17]

Later in 1965, after negotiations among many delegations, the General Assembly adopted a resolution containing guiding principles for the negotiation of a non-proliferation treaty. Among other things, the resolution said that such a treaty "should embody an acceptable balance of mutual responsibilities and obligations of the nuclear and non-nuclear powers" and that it should be a step towards "general and complete disarmament and, more particularly, nuclear disarmament."[18] Thus, the UN resolution, the non-aligned memorandum, and the Italian proposal all called for progress *toward* "nuclear disarmament" even before the steps and conditions necessary for general and complete disarmament had been achieved.

When the Geneva conference resumed in 1966, the debate centered on how to link a non-proliferation treaty with steps toward nuclear disarmament. The Egyptian delegate proposed that a non-proliferation treaty include a "*legal obligation* to halt the nuclear arms race, limit, reduce and eliminate stocks of nuclear weapons and delivery vehicles, and to that end continue and expedite negotiations in order to reach agreement on concrete measures." With such an obligation, he said, countries not having nuclear weapons could judge "objectively" whether sufficient progress had been made by those having them to satisfy the treaty, and they could withdraw from it if progress was so small as to constitute "non-observance."[19]

The Non-Aligned Eight agreed on a new memorandum listing specific proposals for "tangible steps to halt the nuclear arms race and to limit, reduce and eliminate the stocks of nuclear weapons and the means of their delivery." These included a ban on nuclear testing, an end to the production of fissionable material for weapons, and "a freeze and a gradual reduction of the stocks of nuclear weapons and the means of their delivery, the banning of the use of nuclear weapons and assurance of the security of non-nuclear-weapon states." The memorandum added: "Such different steps could be embodied in a treaty as part of its provisions or as a declaration of intention."[20]

In 1967, after the Soviet Union and the United States had resolved many of their differences and submitted identical drafts of a treaty, the Mexican delegation proposed the following article as an amendment:

> Each nuclear-weapon State Party to this Treaty undertakes to pursue negotiations in good faith, with all speed and perseverance, to arrive at further agreements regarding the prohibition of nuclear weapon tests, the cessation of the manufacture of nuclear weapons, the liquidation of their existing stockpiles, the elimination from nuclear arsenals of nuclear weapons and the means of their delivery, as well as to reach agreement on a treaty on general and complete disarmament under strict and effective international control.[21]

This language clearly contemplated that negotiations for the elimination of nuclear weapons from national stockpiles could take place outside the context of general and complete disarmament. Brazil, Burma, India, Romania and Switzerland made somewhat similar proposals—that the treaty contain language obligating the nuclear-weapon powers to "adopt," "take," "resolve . . . to undertake," or "undertake . . . to negotiate" specific steps toward nuclear disarmament.[22] None of these proposals mentioned general and complete disarmament.

Even earlier, U.S. allies considering a U.S.-Soviet draft before it was made public at Geneva had expressed interest in linking non-proliferation obligations to new limitations on the nuclear arms race. The Canadian representative had said: "It is neither unnatural nor unreasonable that countries forgoing their option to produce nuclear weapons should wish to ensure that their act of self-denial should in turn lead the nuclear weapon powers to undertake tangible steps to reduce and eliminate their vast stockpiles of nuclear weapons and delivery vehicles."[23] The Japanese foreign minister had

One route to "nuclear disarmament" was foreseen without preconditions, and another to "general and complete disarmament" with them.

announced that a treaty prohibiting non-proliferation should "go further to make clear the sincere intention on the part of the the countries which possess nuclear weapons to make efforts toward nuclear disarmament . . . ."[24] The British representative had argued that the treaty's terms "must provide the *means of redress* for the non-nuclear powers if the nuclear states are unreasonably slow in translating their intentions ["to halt and reverse" the nuclear arms race] into action."[25] (The "means of redress" commonly mentioned at the Geneva conference were: [1] withdrawal from the NPT by have-nots; [2] meetings of the parties every five years to review the treaty; and [3] a meeting at the end of its initial term to consider how long to extend it.[26])

The Soviet Union and the United States had no choice but to heed these views if they wanted to secure widespread adherence to a non-proliferation treaty. They revised the Mexican language, deleting references to specific measures and proposing what became the obligation in Article VI to negotiate "in good faith on effective measures relating to the cessation of the nuclear arms race at an early date and to nuclear disarmament, and on a treaty on general and complete disarmament . . . ."[27]

They later revised their draft Treaty to offer a review conference every five years of the treaty's life instead of once at the end of the first five. Also, treaty duration was changed from "unlimited" to an initial term of 25 years at the end of which the parties would review whether the treaty's obligations were being observed and decide how much longer it should last.[28]

For Article VI and other obligations, these arrangements provided something akin to enforcement. The negotiators assumed that the Security Council would deal with treaty violations that constituted a threat to the peace because the UN Charter already gave it that authority.[29] However, the five acknowledged nuclear-weapon powers were each permanent members of the Security Council with veto power. No new authority was provided in the NPT to refer disputes over alleged treaty violations to the Security Council, to World Court adjudication, to mediation, or to arbitration. A dissatisfied party could withdraw from the treaty, but that required a report by it to the Security Council stating that its "supreme interests" had been jeopardized by "extraordinary events related to the subject matter of the treaty."[30] Examples could be the development of nuclear explosives by a hostile neighbor or a credible nuclear-weapon threat against its territory or forces by a nuclear-weapon state. From the point of view of the countries not having nuclear weapons, the provisions for conferences to review the implementation of the NPT every five years and to consider its extension after 25 were the most important opportunities available to pressure parties having nuclear weapons to negotiate seriously to limit or eliminate them.

In a statement offering the final NPT text to the General Assembly, the U.S. representative to the United Nations, former U.S. Supreme Court Justice Arthur Goldberg, stated that these added provisions gave Article VI *"further force."* He added:

> My country believes that the *permanent viability* of this treaty will *depend in large measure on our success in the further negotiations contemplated by Article VI* . . . . Following the conclusion of this treaty, my government will, in the spirit of Article VI . . . pursue further disarmament negotiations with redoubled zeal and hope and with promptness . . . . [31]

To many, Article VI's "pursue negotiations in good faith" may seem so vague as to be almost meaningless. In other contexts, however, both national and international courts have given it sufficient meaning to make it an enforceable promise where there is a judicial system that has jurisdiction.[32] In the NPT, as we have seen, that was not offered. But, if those not having nuclear weapons were not satisfied that the five were complying with Article VI, their most important remedies beyond criticism were to frustrate agreement at review conferences every five years and to refuse to vote for a long extension for the NPT in 1995. As we shall see, they have already prevented consensus at two of the four review conferences because they thought the nuclear-weapon parties were not living up to their Article VI obligations.

The Practice of the NPT Parties Pursuant to Article VI

The NPT was opened for signature on July 1, 1968. At the signing, President Johnson announced that, consistent with the NPT's purpose of promoting arms control and disarmament, agreement had been reached with the Soviet Union for negotiations on the limitation and reduction of strategic ballistic missiles and defenses against them.[33] On the same day, the Soviet government issued a memorandum agreeing to negotiate on strategic delivery vehicles and proposing, in addition, negotiation on a list of eight other arms control measures, including "cessation of production of nuclear weapons and the reduction and elimination of stockpiles"—separately from general and complete disarmament.[34]

Later that summer at the Geneva conference, the Soviet Union, the United States, and the other countries present gave meaning to Article VI by agreeing to an agenda of measures that could be discussed there under a heading taken from Article VI's "effective measures relating to the cessation of the nuclear arms race at an early date and to nuclear disarmament." The agenda *under this heading* included "the cessation of testing, the non-use of nuclear weapons, the cessation of production of fissionable materials for weapons use, the cessation of manufacture of weapons, and reduction and subsequent *elimination* of nuclear stockpiles, nuclear free zones, etc." (emphasis added). The "effective measures . . ." heading was first on the agenda. General and complete disarmament was fourth.[35]

Thus, as interpreted by the Geneva conference that had helped negotiate the NPT, negotiations for elimination of nuclear stockpiles pursuant to Article VI could and should take place either under "nuclear disarmament" without the specified pre-conditions, or under general and complete disarmament with them. During the period when tensions had not yet been eased and trust between states had not been strengthened, the more meaningful of these two routes toward the elimination of all nuclear weapons would clearly be the first.

> *In the eyes of the non-nuclear NPT parties, a CTB is the most important measure the nuclear weapon states can adopt.*

This assessment has been reflected in the practice of the parties. The U.S. and U.S.S.R. pursued negotiations bilaterally on their nuclear arsenals, eventually reaching extremely important agreements on reductions. General and complete disarmament, although it has been mentioned on the agenda of the Geneva Conference, was not seriously addressed by the nuclear-weapon states in the 26 years since "agenda item 4" was originally adopted. Complaints about this lack of action have not been prominent in the four NPT review conferences.

Relying in part upon Article VI, more than 160 countries have so far joined the NPT. Among the few that presented special statements to the depositary governments when they joined, the majority mentioned the importance of achieving agreements pursuant to Article VI.[36] At each of the four NPT review conferences held so far, the slow progress of the nuclear powers in implementing Article VI has gotten the most attention of the delegates. Indeed, the failure to negotiate a comprehensive test ban despite both Article VI and a separate preambular paragraph calling for CTB negotiations has been the single most contentious issue. Two of the four review conferences (in 1980 and 1990) broke up without achieving a consensus on any final declaration on the implementation of the NPT because of disagreement over language relating to the failure to negotiate a comprehensive test ban. (By agreement, decisions at these conferences were by consensus.)

By 1975, the SALT I Interim Agreement and the ABM Treaty had been achieved. But the non-aligned parties nevertheless criticized the Soviet Union and the United States for failure to live up to their part of the NPT bargain and achieve more than this. The conference president summarized their views by saying they "rather impatiently await concrete and binding results of on-going bilateral negotiations, aiming at ending the quantitative and qualitative arms race, and reducing substantially the levels of nuclear armaments . . . . The comprehensive test ban is clearly recognized as a most decisive element in these efforts. Article VI must be implemented in letter and spirit."[37] A compromise final declaration was agreed at the last minute containing recommendations on the test ban, on further steps in the SALT process, and on other nuclear arms control measures.[38]

At the 1980 review conference, the non-aligned NPT members prevented a consensus on a final declaration even though serious U.S.-Soviet-U.K. negotiations on ending nuclear testing had made progress. The conference followed the Soviet invasion of Afghanistan and the sharp Western reaction to that invasion. The non-aligned countries again indicated that the nuclear-weapon parties, through their failure to agree on a comprehensive test ban, on bringing the SALT II treaty into force, and on continuing negotiations to achieve substantial reductions in strategic offensive arms, had not kept their end of the NPT bargain.[39]

At the 1985 review conference, there was little new progress pursuant to Article VI to report, but U.S.-Soviet strategic arms negotiations had just begun in Geneva after a long lapse and a Reagan-Gorbachev summit meeting was imminent. After several years of sharpened East-West hostility, the delegates to the conference were reluctant to criticize such hopeful efforts too severely and thus permitted a consensus on a final declaration.

The 1985 conference declaration is of particular interest here, since the language relating to Article VI reflects agreement by the NPT's parties that zero nuclear weapons were to be pursued, but not solely in the context of general and complete disarmament. The declaration summarized with approval the final report of the 1978 special session of the UN General Assembly dealing with disarmament. That report had noted that progress *toward* general and complete disarmament could be taken by specific steps which should be implemented within a few years. It outlined a "Programme of Action" to accomplish such steps without awaiting agreement on general and complete disarmament. This included "a comprehensive, phased programme with agreed time-frames, whenever feasible, for progressive and balanced reduction of stockpiles of nuclear weapons and their means of delivery, leading to *their ultimate and complete elimination at the earliest possible time.*"[40]

To put this in the context of Article VI, the 1985 NPT review conference's final declaration summarized it with approval. NPT parties in 1985 thus agreed that the "phased programme" leading to zero was within the Article VI obligation relating to "nuclear disarmament," not just that relating to general and complete disarmament.[41] The final report also reflected sharp criticism by the non-nuclear-weapon parties of the failure to achieve a nuclear test ban; it also contained this language:

> [T]he Conference noted that certain states Party to the Treaty [understood to mean Britain and the United States], while committed to the goal of an effectively verifiable comprehensive Nuclear Test-Ban Treaty, considered *deep and verifiable reductions in existing arsenals of nuclear weapons* as the highest priority in the process of pursuing the objectives of Article VI.[42]

This clearly implied that deep cuts in nuclear weapons could and should be negotiated outside the context of general and complete disarmament (as was later done in START I and START II).

By the time of the 1990 review conference, there had been successful Reagan-Gorbachev summits, an end to the Cold War, agreement on an Intermediate-Range Nuclear Force (INF) treaty, and progress toward the first START treaty. Both of these treaties were intended to reduce nuclear delivery vehicles, but both had or would have the additional effect of withdrawing nuclear warheads from active deployment. However, in 1990 a consensus final declaration again proved elusive, owing primarily to the failure of the nuclear powers to achieve a test ban. Mexico, the leader of the non-aligned countries, refused to accept a compromise such as that of 1985—a compromise that would have criticized the failure to achieve a test ban pursuant to Article VI, but also would have reflected views of Britain and the United States such as those quoted above.[43]

Conclusions on the Meaning of Article VI

1. Article VI said that measures relating to "cessation of the nuclear arms race at an early date" were to be negotiated when the treaty entered into force (1970). The three such measures most often mentioned in the negotiating history and in the parties' 1968 agreement on an agenda to implement Article VI were a ban on nuclear testing; a cut-off in the production of fissionable materials for nuclear weapons; and a prohibition on the use of nuclear weapons.

After almost 25 years, none of these measures has been achieved in internationally binding form. There exist four-power, reciprocal moratoria on testing (China being the sole holdout), a U.S.-Soviet Threshold Test Ban Treaty, unilateral cut-offs of fissionable-material production for weapons by the United States and soon by Russia, and national declarations promising not to use nuclear weapons on non-nuclear-weapon countries by each of the five prowers—with differences in their coverage.[44] Negotiations for multilateral treaties covering all three measures—to end tests and production of material for weapons and to ban their use with agreed exceptions—are now on the agenda of the Conference on Disarmament (CD) in Geneva. But agreements since 1970 in the "cessation-of-the-nuclear-arms-race" category are quite few.

The five countries accepted by the NPT as nuclear-weapon states have a clear Article VI obligation to negotiate in good faith on all three of these measures at Geneva. The measures have greater urgency under Article VI than measures relating to "nuclear disarmament"—though they are not required to be completed before an obligation to negotiate toward nuclear disarmament arises.

Three of the five nuclear-weapon powers—Britain, the Soviet Union (now Russia) and the United States—participated in the last serious test ban negotiations ending in 1980. All five are members of the multilateral CD in Geneva, but China and France (also members of the CD) were not obliged to negotiate in good faith on "cessation-of-the-nuclear-arms-race" measures until they joined the NPT in 1992.

Until this year, there had been little recent discussion in the CD about a cut-off in the production of fissile material for nuclear weapons. However, a 1993 UN General Assembly resolution on such a cut-off, new support from the United States, and the joint US-Russian statement of January 14, 1994—in which both powers "expressed their resolve to implement effective measures to limit and reduce nuclear weapons" and announced that "an important contribution to the goal of non-proliferation of nuclear weapons would be made by a verifiable ban on the production of fissile materials for nuclear weapons and by the most rapid conclusion of an international convention to this effect"—may all give impetus to that subject.[45] At the beginning of its 1994 session, the CD appointed a Special Coordinator (a representative of Canada) to consult the other parties on the scope and forum for negotiating "a non-discriminatory, multilateral and internationally and effectively verifiable treaty banning the production of fissile material for nuclear weapons or other nuclear explosive devices."

There have been no American or Russian plans to go to zero nuclear weapons. The NPT requires more than this.

Disagreement over exceptions to an obligation not to use nuclear weapons against non-nuclear-weapon states has prevented agreement on a treaty on the non-use of nuclear weapons at Geneva for years.[46] However, new efforts are likely in view of both the upcoming 1995 NPT review and extension conference and the need of assurances to persuade Ukraine to release the nuclear weapons left on its territory when it declared independence.[47] In the January 14, 1994 trilateral statement signed in Moscow by the presidents of Russia, United States, and Ukraine, the first two agreed to give Ukraine identical security assurances as soon as it accedes to the NPT. Thus all three measures (CTB, cut-off, and security assurances) will, in all likelihood, receive new attention during 1994.

2. Of the three "cessation-of-the-nuclear-arms-race" measures, the comprehensive test ban has always been mentioned as a first-order priority; recall that it alone is specified in the preamble of the NPT.[48] At the preceding four NPT review conferences, the failure to achieve a CTB received the greatest attention and was the reason two of the four conferences adjourned without agreement on a final declaration. In the eyes of the NPT parties not having nuclear weapons, there is no question that a CTB is the most important measure the nuclear-weapon states can adopt in satisfying their Article VI obligations.

There will be two important differences at the 1995 conference from past NPT review conferences. The first is that a failure to reach agreement at the 1995 conference could mean an end to the NPT. For the first time, the NPT parties not having nuclear weapons will possess real bargaining leverage vis-à-vis the nuclear powers to push for a test ban. Realizing their leverage, the non-aligned members of the Geneva CD issued a statement on December 1, 1993 in which they demanded achievment of a "final text" of a CTBT during 1994.[49]

The second difference is that the decision on the length of the NPT extension will be made by majority voting, not by the consensus procedure of the review conferences. This is especially significant since the parties will be asked to decide the treaty's term of renewal, not just to comment on the treaty's performance. Moreover, this important conference decision cannot be blocked by a small minority as was the case with decisions at past review conferences.

What impact will these changes have on the prospects for achieving a test ban? NPT parties seeking such a ban would certainly not get what they want by bringing the NPT to an end. Moreover, all or most of the developing countries that are among the strongest advocates of a test ban have an interest in continuing the NPT as long as it is seen as effective in preventing other countries from securing nuclear weapons and in promoting trade in nuclear material and equipment under safeguards.[50] But given the failure of the nuclear-weapon countries to achieve a test ban for 25 years, the developing countries may not trust them to agree on a CTB without exerting strong pressure on them to do so.

One developing-country proposal to deal with this dilemma could be to extend the NPT in 1995 for a short period, perhaps two years, in order to provide more time for test ban negotiations, and then to extend it for a longer period if a test ban has been achieved. There are, however, serious doubts about the legality of this proposal, and the result of a two-year extension could well be an end to the NPT in 1997.[51]

A more likely alternative of the non-nuclear parties could be to call for a recess of the 1995 conference, perhaps for six months, with the idea of reconvening it to make the extension decision once a test ban has been achieved.[52] Since the non-aligned countries constitute some two-thirds of the NPT's membership, they have it within their power to precipitate such a recess if they cooperate. Moreover, since preventing proliferation depends so heavily on the consent of all the countries capable of building nuclear weapons, the proponents of a long NPT extension are unlikely to press their proposal to a vote in 1995 unless they have a substantial majority. Having nuclear-capable countries going home mad from the conference and threatening withdrawal from the NPT would be an unhealthy result.[53] Given the interest of almost all the NPT parties in preventing the NPT from lapsing after a short (two years?) extension, a recess of the 1995 conference until a test ban is negotiated seems quite possible if no test ban text has been agreed to by the opening of the conference.[54]

3. Turning to Article VI measures "relating to . . . nuclear disarmament," the Soviet Union and the United States have implemented the INF treaty eliminating their intermediate-range nuclear forces. In the START I and II treaties, Russia and the United States have agreed on deep cuts down to at least 3,500 warheads each in their strategic nuclear forces. By reciprocal action, Russia and the United States have deactivated, withdrawn, or dismantled many nuclear warheads of all ranges, including many not covered by the INF and START treaties. These are major achievements in compliance with

the obligation of Article VI to negotiate in good faith on measures "relating to . . . nuclear disarmament."

So far, the other three nuclear-weapon parties, Britain, China and France, have not participated in the American-Soviet (now Russian) negotiations to reduce nuclear weapons. China and France did not become obligated to do so until they joined the NPT in 1992, but they will surely need to talk about nuclear reductions with the other nuclear-weapon powers before the 1995 conference opens to demonstrate compliance with Article VI.

Russia and the United States have not yet had any serious negotiations on going below the final START II levels of land-based and sea-based strategic missile warheads—levels *higher* than what existed on both sides in 1970 when the NPT went into effect.[55] Furthermore, except for 30-year old plans for general and complete disarmament and a Gorbachev proposal of 1986 to eliminate nuclear weapons by the year 2000, there have been no specific American or Russian national plans for going to zero—much less talks between the two or among the five toward that end. Article VI clearly requires more than this.

4. The NPT's preambular language dealing with general and complete disarmament suggests that "easing of international tensions and the strengthening of international trust between states" was thought necessary in 1968 to facilitate the "elimination from national arsenals of nuclear weapons and the means of their delivery." Even if these pre-conditions must be met not just for "general and complete disarmament," but also for "nuclear disarmament," the fear of a U.S.-Russian nuclear exchange has receded greatly with the end of the Cold War. That has eased East-West tensions. However, the world remains a dangerous place. Regional conflicts, ethnic violence, nationalistic separatism and civil wars have in fact increased since the Cold War's end. The peaceful world necessary as a prerequisite for deep cuts in conventional armaments has not yet arrived, the UN has not yet shown itself capable enough of handling violent disputes, and general and complete disarmament still does not seem to be realistic.

But the plain meaning of Article VI, its negotiating history, and the parties' practice in implementing it all suggest that these pre-conditions do not need to be satisfied to trigger an obligation to negotiate in good faith toward zero nuclear weapons along the "nuclear disarmament" route. After 25 years and an end to the Cold War, the time has been reached when Article VI requires all five nuclear-weapon states to begin such talks. Article VI does not say whether negotiating toward zero means taking one step downward after another through one negotiation after another, or a "phased programme" involving a package of steps agreed in one long nego-tiation. At the same time, Article VI does not authorize an avoidance of negotiations by any of the five just because the Americans and Russians have agreed to reduce to 3,500 strategic warheads. Indeed, all five nuclear powers have a present, pressing obligation to begin discussing proposals for moving in the direction of zero along one route or the other. [56]

ANNEX

An Article VI Negotiating Forum of "Five Plus One"

James F. Leonard

Introduction

There may be room for debate on exactly what the nuclear-weapon states agreed to in Article VI of the NPT, but it certainly cannot be plausibly argued that they have done all that they are obligated to do. Some further constraints on nuclear weapons are clearly in order. The U.S. and Russia have done quite a bit, especially if the unratified START I and II treaties and the unilateral withdrawals of tactical nuclear weapons are taken into account. Yet START II will leave the two major powers seven to ten years from now with more strategic weapons than when the NPT was negotiated. The U.S.-Soviet arms race may have ended, but it has left an enormous "overhang" that must be cleaned up.

The United Kingdom, France, and China are even more plainly not yet in compliance with Article VI, despite their much lower stockpiles. None of the three has engaged itself to any significant limitation of the size or character of its nuclear arsenal. France and China only recently adhered to the NPT, but neither made any reservation with regard to Article VI when they joined the treaty, and their silence leaves them bound by it. Chinese spokesmen, in fact, are constantly calling for the complete elimination of nuclear weapons, but the Chinese government has made no proposals as to how that goal should be attained.

The obvious way for the nuclear powers to comply with Article VI is to establish a negotiating forum, including at least the five declared nuclear-weapon states. The obvious government to initiate the establishment of such a forum is the United States, today by far the most powerful of the five. And the obvious incentive for the U.S. to do so is to assist in securing its announced objective of an indefinite, unconditional extension of the NPT in 1995.

A Five Plus One Forum

Some have suggested a larger forum than the five, perhaps including the three threshold states—Israel, India, and Pakistan—and even some non-nuclear states like Sweden, Germany, or Japan. These are not good ideas. The "threshold three" are regional, not global problems, despite India's assertion of a China rationale for its nuclear program. These problems should be dealt with separately; much later, when the five are reducing to very low levels, there will be a need to bring them into an eventual universal system of nuclear arms control. They should, of course, continue to participate in the CTB and impending fissile-material negotiations.

The rationale for bringing committed, sophisticated non-nuclear governments like Sweden into an Article VI negotiating forum would be "to keep the five honest." That is a reasonable concern, since there are important elements in all five who oppose nuclear arms control and consider elimination a dangerous fantasy. If not closely monitored, these elements will find ways to drag five-power negotiations out for many, many years.

The proper way to monitor the negotiations is not, however, to have one or more non-nuclear state present at the table, but to have an international presence there—be it a representative of the UN or the Conference on Disarmament (CD). This would effectively symbolize and represent the interest of the entire international community in the successful prosecution of five-power talks.

The UN or CD representative would not be a negotiating party; indeed his mandate should be to remain silent and listen. At prescribed intervals this representative should report, publicly, on the developments in the talks. These reports would provide a basis for political assessments by governments, perhaps periodically in the CD and annually at the General Assembly, or perhaps in the Security Council.

Nothing, of course, could or should prevent the five governments from communicating with each other behind the back of the international observer; nothing, that is, except the certainty that such "back channel" talks would eventually become public knowledge, and if they were discreditable, it would bring discredit on those involved.

Some will object that negotiations conducted entirely in public can never succeed. The objection has merit. Governments need ways to try out ideas before they become fully committed to them, but that is utterly different from colluding behind the scenes to prevent any progress from being made. A UN or CD observer, if he gains the trust of the parties, can in fact become one of several channels that are always available for "trial balloons." What an international presence and public reporting *can* do is to deter to some degree the launching of formal proposals that are so one-sided or so unrealistic that they give rise to ridicule or indignation. Over the years, the super-secret U.S.-Soviet bilaterals were the scene of entirely too much of that sort of thing.

To get this Five Plus One negotiation under way, a formal initiative, preferably from the U.S., should lead to convening a five-power preparatory group charged with developing a mandate and presenting it to some larger forum for comment. The CD in Geneva looks like the logical locus for this operation. The mandate, as modified, could then be approved by the General Assembly in late 1994 or the NPT Extension Conference in early 1995. The Five Plus One negotiating forum could then be formally opened concurrently with or just following the NPT Extension Conference.

A Negotiating Agenda and Mandate

The first item on the agenda of this Article VI forum might well be the transparency, safety and security of the five existing stockpiles. Even before they begin serious talks on reductions, they should seek ways to reassure each other—and the entire world—that another Chernobyl raised to the nth power is not smoldering some-where in a missile silo or storage igloo. Such a discussion will natu-rally lead toward international monitoring of stockpiles *and* deployed forces. The security assurances which one can hope will have been articulated by that time will, through these safety and transparency measures, gain a credibility and a political significance which mere declarations would never command.

Putting security and transparency up front as a rationale for the Article VI talks will build support for them in defense establish-ments, which would otherwise tend to be reserved, if not hostile. In fact, it might lead to an early exploration of the subject among the five during the period before formal negotiations can get under way. Finally, the launching of a U.S. initiative addressed to the other four, if supported strongly by Russia, could put a much better foun-dation under our joint efforts in Kiev, where there is a steady refrain asking why Ukrainian weapons are thought so dangerous while French and British weapons seem to cause no concern.

The mandate for Article VI negotiations will certainly have to ad-dress force levels and not only transparency. Reaffirmation of the goal of eventual elimination will obviously be required. Anything that looks like weakening that commitment and making permanent the division of the world into nuclear "haves" and "have-nots" would be a grave, perhaps even fatal blow to the non-proliferation regime. But mere reaffirmation of this goal of elimi-nation is not likely to satisfy the more activist members of the NPT, egged on by at least India from outside. The non-nuclear-weapon states will recog-nize that elimination is at best years, even decades, away; however, they will want to see some sort of program for how the five plan to move through the disarmament process toward that goal.

> *Advancing security and transpar-ency as a rationale for Article VI talks will build support for them in defense establishments.*

An early commitment in the security portion of the five-power agenda to "zero alert" could help in this regard. It is an easily understood concept: the de-activization of all nuclear forces on "hair-trigger" alert status, and the introduction of internationally monitored delay arrangements into all deployments. But it is not a simple matter to move from the concept to the design and negotiation of such arrangements. Moreover, the "zero alert" concept does not in itself necessarily entail any force reductions and thus cannot symbolize the required commitment to move "in the direction of nuclear disarmament," as the NPT urges.

To persuade the non-nuclear states to take seriously the political will of the nuclear states to make the Five Plus One talks "real" and thus to fulfill their Article VI commitment, some intermediate goal of force levels may be needed. The START II level of 3,000–3,500 deployed weapons (implying stocks of around 5,000 weapons each) is simply too high. Not only is it above the strategic deployment levels of 1968 when the NPT was concluded, but it is so far above the U.K., French, and Chinese levels that it exerts no political pressure on them to join in a reduction process.

An intermediate goal of 1,000 deployed weapons for the U.S. and Russia would be a useful concept around which a political consensus could be constructed. It would entail a serious and difficult negotiation between Washington and Moscow over the major force restructuring involved in going from 3,000 to 1,000. The U.S., at least, would have to re-study yet again its targeting doctrine and thus ask itself the basic question of what purposes its nuclear weapons really serve.

A cap of 1,000 on the deployed weapons of any nuclear power would not involve any reductions in the U.K. or French forces or plans. That is probably true for China as well. The two major powers, supported by the rest of the world, could reasonably propose that in return for such major reductions in their forces, the other three should accept a lower cap, say 500 deployed weapons. The Chinese might argue that because they have no nuclear allies, they should not be asked to accept a lower cap than Russia, which also stands alone in this sense.

However this number game might play out during the drafting of the mandate for the Article VI negotiations or in the opening phase of the actual negotiations, it will be important to retain the concept that it is the U.S.-Russian *acceptance* of the intermediate goal of 1,000 weapons, not the *attainment* of that goal, that will trigger acceptance by the other three of caps of 500 weapons (or whatever number is settled on) *and the initiation of negotiations* on verifying those caps. The opening of serious five-power discussions on limiting all five nuclear arsenals should be attainable around or shortly after the NPT extension conference, not at some vague date in the next century when the two major powers have gone through their bilateral negotiations on how to reach the lower levels and then have carried out the required de-activizations and dismantlements. What the non-nuclear states will rightly demand is five power negotiations starting *now*, in the same time frame if not at the same moment that they are committing themselves to the extension of the NPT.

2.
Two Options for the 1995 NPT Extension Conference Revisited

George Bunn and Charles N. Van Doren

Introduction

This article revisits two options for extending the nuclear Non-Proliferation Treaty (NPT) in 1995 that we considered in 1991 in "Options for Extension of the NPT: The Intention of the Drafters of Article X.2."[1] The 1991 study concluded that if the 1995 conference became stalemated—or "hung"—because no majority could agree on any particular period of extension, the NPT would continue provisionally until the NPT parties could agree. The study also concluded that a valid extension option was extension of the treaty for an indefinite number of fixed periods of equal length, one succeeding another automatically unless, before the end of one of these periods, a majority of the parties decided to terminate the treaty.

The purpose of revisiting these two options is that important State Department telegrams dealing with the 1960s negotiation of the pertinent treaty language have been declassified and have become available since the time of our analysis in 1991. An additional purpose of revisiting these options is that several questions have been raised about our "hung-conference" conclusions, particularly by Professor Serge Sur, an international lawyer and Deputy Director of the United Nations Institute for Disarmament Research (UNIDIR).[2]

The pertinent NPT language is found in Article X.2:

> Twenty-five years after the entry into force of the Treaty [i.e., in 1995], a conference shall be convened to decide whether the Treaty shall continue in force *indefinitely, or shall be extended for an additional fixed period or periods*. This decision shall be taken by a majority of the Parties to the Treaty. (Emphasis added.)

1. The Hung Conference

What happens if disagreement at the 1995 conference prevents any majority from forming for any particular extension, either for an "additional fixed period," successive "additional fixed . . . periods" or "indefinitely?"

Our 1991 paper concludes that in the event of a hung conference, the NPT would continue provisionally until the parties could reach agreement on a particular extension. Given that the purpose of the 1995 conference is to choose between an indefinite extension or one for a fixed period or periods, it would make little sense to have the treaty come to an abrupt end before that choice was made. Our analysis relied upon the treaty's language, its negotiating history and on the interpretation of a somewhat similar provision by the Court of Justice of the European Community.[3]

Professor Sur argued that "indefinite extension of the Treaty in the absence of a positive decision of the kind envisaged in Article X.2 leads to absurd consequences."[4] If Sur interprets "indefinite" to mean that it "shall continue in force indefinitely," then we concur. Otherwise, by failing to make a choice, the parties would have chosen one of the extension options explicitly provided for in Article VIII of the treaty. However, our analysis does not use the word "indefinite." Indeed, the judicial opinion of the Court of Justice of the European Community involved a similar dispute, and in that instance it was determined that pending a further decision the treaty provisions in question would continue "provisionally."

The differences between our argument and Professor Sur are therefore not as wide as might be perceived. Indeed, Sur agrees with much of what we say. His analysis states that:

> "It is clear that so long as a decision is not taken, the NPT remains in force. It is not automatically terminated at the end of the 25-year period envisaged in Article X.2, but lapses only if the conference fails."

We disagree with the conclusion that the NPT lapses if the conference fails to reach any extension decision. As David Fischer points out, the result of Sur's conclusion could be that if insufficient time and funds were provided by the conference's organizers, the NPT could lapse abruptly—an option not envisioned in the treaty's language and certainly not intended by the parties should they fail to agree on any extension option.[5] Reconvening the conference to "try again," however, would be consistent with the language of the treaty.

International law attempts to discourage the arbitrary termination of treaties. The Vienna Convention on the Law of Treaties permits the "termination of a treaty or the withdrawal of a party" from a treaty in only two circumstances relevant here: "(a) in conformity with the provisions of the treaty, or (b) at any time by consent of all the parties" after consultation with the other parties.[6] There are a few other circumstances permitting withdrawal from treaty obligations, including, for example, material breach by another party. None of these, however, seem applicable in the case of the NPT.[7] By hypothesis, the pertinent alternative to treaty-authorized termination in the Vienna Convention, i.e. "consent of all the parties," would not be relevant, since a majority of the parties cannot be mustered to end the treaty immediately.

Our 1991 paper concludes that in the event of a hung conference, the NPT would continue provisionally.

In addition to Article X.2 quoted above, other NPT provisions authorize termination of the treaty or withdrawal of a party. There is an explicit provision for withdrawal by individual parties in Article X.1 if they state that "extraordinary events, related to the subject matter of this Treaty, have jeopardized [their] supreme interests" and give notice to this effect to the UN Security Council, among others. There is also an article providing a procedure for amendments (Article VIII). An amendment, though difficult to accomplish, could end the treaty or ameliorate a party's dissatisfaction with it. Finally, there is an article authorizing review of the treaty by the parties every five years (Article VIII.3). While not itself providing a method for ending the treaty, a review conference could help build a consensus for termination by a decision of the 1995 conference, by withdrawal because of "extraordinary events . . . ," or because of material breach of the treaty by a party.

With all of these treaty outlets available for parties to express their dissatisfaction, the NPT could hardly have been intended to end for all parties simply because the first convening of an extension conference could not reach a decision. Indeed, the history of the negotiations suggests otherwise. The Vienna Convention on the Law of Treaties authorizes resort to this history, that is, to the "preparatory work of the treaty and the circumstances of its conclusion," in order to confirm the meaning derived from reading its text, or to derive the true meaning of the treaty if the text is "ambiguous or obscure."[8] Thus, whether the text is clear or obscure, the negotiating history is relevant.

At the time of the negotiations, the Soviet Union and the United States co-chaired the multilateral Geneva disarmament conference (then called the Eighteen-Nation Disarmament Committee) and were expected to provide most of the treaty drafts for comment by other conference members.[9] Both provided drafts that called explicitly for a treaty of indefinite or unlimited duration rather than a fixed term of a specified number of years. However, the countries that were most advanced in civilian nuclear technology, including those relying on an alliance with the United States to deter possible attack by the Soviet Union, objected to an NPT of longer duration than their alliances might turn out to be. Germany and Italy were particularly vocal in this regard.[10]

Whether the text is clear or obscure, the negotiating history is relevant.

To achieve an agreement, the U.S. negotiator, Adrian Fisher, recommended privately to Washington in 1966 the elimination of the language in the American draft that: "[T]his treaty shall be of unlimited duration." Instead, Fisher would have substituted:

> This treaty shall remain in force for (five) (ten) years after its entry into force. Six months prior to the expiration of this period, a conference of the parties shall be held in Geneva, Switzerland in order to decide whether the treaty shall be extended.[11]

Neither Washington nor Moscow was prepared in 1966 to give up on unlimited duration, and it was not then proposed to the Geneva conference by either government. During 1967, however, Germany, Italy and several neutral and non-aligned countries expressed disagreement with unlimited duration. For some time before Fisher's recommendation, Italy had been proposing parallel unilateral declarations by non-nuclear-weapon countries not to acquire nuclear weapons. These declarations were to be for a fixed period of years to be followed by consultations among the declarant on what to do next; they were to be terminable by any declarant if another acquired nuclear weapons.[12] In late 1967, Italy offered an alternative to these declarations, which would have produced similar flexibility in the NPT. The Italian delegate proposed eliminating "unlimited duration" in the NPT draft and substituting:

> The present treaty shall have a duration of X years. It shall be *automatically* extended for *terms equal to its initial duration* for those governments which, *subject to six months notice*, shall not have made known their intention to withdraw. (Emphasis added.)[13]

Just before this text was offered publicly to the Geneva conference, but after consulting with the Italian delegate, Adrian Fisher again privately recommended to Washington that the U.S. approve a fixed-term duration clause. His proposal:

> Twenty-five years after the entry into force of the Treaty, a conference shall be convened to decide whether the treaty shall continue in force indefinitely, or shall be extended for an additional fixed period or periods. This decision shall be taken by a majority of the parties to the treaty. [Within six months after the conclusion of the conference, any party may give the depositary governments formal written notice of its intention to denounce the treaty. Such denunciation shall take effect three months from the date of receipt by the depositary governments of the written notice.][14]

The first two sentences of Fisher's recommendation are the present NPT text; as explained in the next section of this paper, the bracketed two recommendations were deleted following objections by the Soviet delegation. It is instructive to compare this draft language with Fisher's earlier draft. Why, for example, did he add "indefinitely" and "additional fixed period or periods?"

Clearly, Fisher was attempting to gain Italian and other support for the treaty by eliminating "unlimited duration" and instead providing for a fixed-year initial term with the possibility of repeated renewals. By doing so, he also would have met Italy's desire for an easy withdrawal opportunity, providing for six months notice at the end of the initial term. His telegram expressed his desire to meet the "political needs FRG [Germany], GOI [Italy] and possibly also Japan" to win their acceptance of the NPT.[15]

At the same time, Fisher was trying to meet the Soviet and American desire for a treaty of long duration by calling for a twenty-five year term rather than the five- or ten-year term that he had recommended to Washington earlier, and by providing for the possibility of an indefinite extension after twenty-five years—or at least successive renewals for "additional fixed . . . periods." In his telegram to Washington, Fisher conceded that a treaty of unlimited duration, even if providing for an easy withdrawal after twenty-five years, would be preferable "from U.S., as well as Soviet, standpoint . . . under ideal circumstances."[16] In a later telegram, he repeated that the Soviet Union would "want the longest possible period."[17] However, in both telegrams, Fisher recommended his draft as a compromise designed to gain the agreement of the Italians (and those for whom they spoke), as well as the Soviets and his own government.[18]

Fisher's draft was arguably not intended to produce a treaty having a twenty-five year duration with no provision for further extension. His telegram suggested that the language in the then current U.S. draft calling for "unlimited duration" would be deleted if his recommendation was accepted: "Without this sentence," he added, the "treaty will automatically be of *unlimited duration* unless otherwise stipulated [in the treaty] or unless review conference takes *positive* decision to make treaty limited."[19] Fisher had been chief legal adviser to the U.S. State Department and the chief reporter for the *Restatement of the Law (2nd): The Foreign Relations Law of the United States.*[20] As his telegram indicates, Fisher recognized that treaties ordinarily continue unless their language provides otherwise or unless all the parties agree to terminate them.[21] (See the discussion of

> U.S. negotiator Adrian Fisher recommended his draft to gain the agreement of the Italians (and those for whom they spoke).

the Vienna Convention provisions on termination above.) Thus, under Fisher's text, in the absence of a "positive decision" of the extension conference, the treaty would continue until such a decision could be made. Later, the Egyptian delegate, an advocate of unlimited duration, told the Geneva conference publicly that his government could agree to the new duration clause "if it is generally supported and cannot in any way make possible the termination of the treaty twenty-five years after its entry into force."[22] No other delegate speaking at the conference argued that the compromise meant a twenty-five year term without the opportunity to extend the treaty.

Taken together, this information tends to confirm the conclusion that the treaty would continue provisionally in the event of a "hung conference" until a majority of the parties could agree on some form of extension.

2. Successive Extensions of Equal Length

Could the 1995 extension conference extend the NPT for an indefinite number of fixed periods of equal length, each succeeding the other automatically unless, toward the end of one of these periods, a majority decided against continuation of the treaty beyond the end of that period?

The NPT text that we rely upon to answer this question affirmatively is "additional fixed . . . periods." The treaty does not say explicitly that this text means equal periods, but the treaty certainly does not exclude that option. It does not explicitly say that a vote may be taken during each period; however, some action would be necessary to give meaning to the distinction in Article X.2 between "additional fixed period" and "additional fixed . . . periods," and between the latter of these options and "indefinitely." Otherwise, there would be no difference between one seventy-five year extension and three successive twenty-five year extensions, or between indefinite duration and an indefinite number of consecutive renewals of twenty-five years each. To give meaning to the plural "periods" as a discrete option, there would need to be the possibility of some significant action before the end of each of the "periods." The action having the greatest significance to the parties would be a vote, and the extension conference language calls for a majority vote at the end of the first twenty-five period. Thus, the opportunity for such a vote toward the end of each of the "additional fixed . . . periods" fits with the logic of the language.

If this seems persuasive, then the negotiating history is equally so. As noted in the first section, Adrian Fisher's draft language for Article X.2 was heavily influenced by the Italian proposals for unilateral non-acquisition declarations for a fixed number of years, followed by consultation and an opportunity for easy withdrawal. Another form of this idea was Italy's proposal for amendment of the NPT (referred to above), stating that after "X" years, the treaty "shall be *automatically* extended for *terms equal to its initial duration* for those governments which, subject to six months notice, shall not have made known their intention to withdraw." (Emphasis added.)

After Fisher was authorized by Washington to forward his revision of the Italian proposal to the Soviets, they returned with instructions to agree to the first two sentences, i.e. the present text, if the United States would agree to omit the last two.[23] As we have noted, those sentences to be omitted read: "Within six months after the conclusion of the conference [called for by the first two sentences], any party may give to the depositary governments formal written notice of its intention to denounce the treaty. Such denunciation shall take effect three months from the date of receipt by the depositary governments of the written notice."[24]

If "additional fixed . . . periods" includes automatic renewal, then this would have given Italy much of what they were after: a limited-term followed by automatic renewals, but with the opportunity at the end of twenty-five years to withdraw without stating any reason.

According to Fisher's reporting cable, the Soviets privately rejected these two sentences saying that:

> They have gone 99 percent of the way to meet U.S. by eliminating references to the treaty being of unlimited duration, by providing for a conference after 25 years, which can, in effect, terminate the treaty by a majority vote [i.e., by providing only a very short extension]. They also point out that the retention of the existing [withdrawal] clause permits withdrawal by a national decision on the basis of extraordinary events jeopardizing supreme interests. They feel this gives adequate protection. They take quite strongly the position that the last two sentences of the U.S. article which

provides for an additional right of denunciation without any stated reason after the conference has been held and after a majority had voted to extend the treaty would have a destabilizing effect.[25]

As a result, Fisher's language covering the Italian notion of renewal for "additional fixed . . . periods" was left in the treaty, but the opportunity for easy withdrawal after twenty-five years was dropped. When the draft was made public at the Geneva conference, Fisher asserted that the twenty-five year term had been substituted for unlimited duration, but added that the conference at the end of twenty-five years would "decide how much longer the treaty should continue."[26] The three options for the extension conference—indefinite extension, or for an "additional fixed period or periods"—were not discussed at any great length in Geneva. However, the suggestion for an indefinite number of successive renewals for the same fixed period was known to the delegates from several Italian interventions and amendments.[27] Clearly, that option must have been one of the options contemplated under "additional fixed . . . periods."

Later, the idea of periodic conferences was incorporated into the provision for review which, until then, had authorized only one review conference at the end of the first five years. In explaining that additional reviews would provide greater flexibility for those nations dissatisfied with how the NPT was operating, Soviet Ambassador Alexei Roshchin pointed out to the conference that Egypt, Italy, Mexico, Poland and Sweden had asked for periodic review.[28] In his statement to the conference, ACDA Director William C. Foster added:

> We have not felt it advisable to add the further amendment suggested by the representative of Italy, which would give parties a right to denounce [withdraw from] the treaty at the end of twenty-five years without stating any reason therefor. But the provision for periodic review now included in the text does, we believe, encompass the essential element of flexibility which we understand was also in part the aim of the Italian delegation's proposal for amending the duration clause.[29]

If any delegate had been in doubt about the influence of the Italian model for the duration provision, that uncertainty was removed by Foster's statement. The conference statements by Italy, the U.S., the Soviet Union, Egypt, Mexico, Poland and Sweden, etc. were of course available to all conference members in Geneva, and to all members of the United Nations when the conference records were sent to New York with the conference report. Moreover, the idea of periodic (every five years) review conferences had attracted considerable interest at the Geneva disarmament conference. Further, since periodic conferences were not limited to the first twenty-five years, the new language permits renewal for successive additional fixed periods (assuming at least five years each), as well as extension for an indefinite term. While not the only option permitted by "additional fixed...periods," the 1995 extension can clearly extend the NPT for an indefinite number of fixed periods of equal length, each succeeding another automatically unless, before the end of any such period, a majority decides against continuation of the treaty beyond that period.

Conclusion

This paper considered two of the several options for dealing with the NPT at the extension conference to be held in 1995. A decision to extend the treaty for an indefinite number of equal fixed periods, each succeeding another subject to a vote at the end of each period, should be very attractive to those NPT members desiring a long-term extension, but who are unwilling to support an extension of the treaty for an unlimited period. This is because the succeeding fixed periods option would afford states with an opportunity to vote whether to continue the treaty for another term when the prior term expired. Members that do not want to commit themselves indefinitely, but nevertheless want to extend the treaty for an additional term without deciding in 1995 that the treaty should end at the end of that term would have an opportunity to do so. At the same time, members who want an unlimited extension could achieve this result in a *de facto* way, subject to their ability to persuade a majority at the end of each twenty-five year period that another twenty-five years should be permitted. Thus, a decision to successively renew twenty-five year periods subject to repeated majority votes could be the compromise that a majority could support in 1995. However, if there is no majority for any of the several options, then the treaty would continue provisionally until a majority of the parties could agree.

Arms build-up 'breached anti-nuclear treaty'

Antony Barnett
Public Affairs Editor

BRITAIN has covertly built up its nuclear arsenal in what anti-nuclear campaigners claim is a clear breach of its obligations under international peace treaties.

An official government report obtained by *The Observer* details how since 1978 British governments have made more than 500 transfers of 'civilian' nuclear material to the Ministry of Defence. In 1968 Britain was one of 62 countries which signed the Nuclear Non-Proliferation Treaty (NPT), which was aimed at stopping such transfers.

Nations with nuclear weapons, such as the UK and the United States, have led international criticism of other countries for trying to develop atomic bombs by using nuclear material from civilian sources.

The imposition of international inspectors on Iraq was based on alleged breaches of the NPT.

The report, released by the Department of Trade and Industry, describes how in 1992 five tons of low-enriched uranium from British Nuclear Fuels' Capenhurst reactor in Cheshire was used to produce tritium, an important component of nuclear weapons manufactured at Aldermaston in Berkshire.

In 1983 almost 100 tons of low-enriched uranium from Capenhurst was used for nuclear weapons material.

The report also gives details of a previously undisclosed incident in 1986 when more than 800 grams of weapons-grade plutonium from BNFL's nuclear reprocessing plant at Sellafield in Cumbria was 'inadvertently' sent to another reactor.

In addition large amounts of depleted uranium from civilian reactors were used for conventional military purposes in making depleted uranium shells and armour for tanks.

Dr David Lowry, an environment consultant who has campaigned for years for the information to be released, said: 'It appears to be a case of one rule for us and another for other countries.'

A Department of Trade and Industry spokesman denied Britain had been guilty of any such breach.

...during the festival. The service also has all the details of how to get to Edinburgh, where to stay, what to eat, where to drink. In fact everything you need to get the most out of the Festival.

3.
Strengthening Nuclear Non-Proliferation
Security Assurances for Non-Nuclear Weapon States

George Bunn

In 1995, a conference of the parties to the Treaty of the Non-Proliferation of Nuclear Weapons (NPT) will meet to decide by majority vote whether to extend that treaty and, if so, for how long. Since the NPT is the foundation of U.S. efforts to prevent the spread of nuclear-weapons-manufacturing capability to additional countries all around the world, extending the treaty indefinitely is very much in the U.S. interest. An important vehicle for making a vote for such an extension acceptable to many non-nuclear-weapon countries would be to provide them with some assurance that their security will be protected should they continue to observe their obligation under the NPT to forswear nuclear weapons.

Towards that end, this paper recommends that the U.S. support a new United Nations (UN) Security Council *resolution* (a) condemning the threat of or use of nuclear weapons against countries that have forsworn them, (b) recognizing that nuclear blackmail or use against such a country would justify Security Council action, and (c) calling for immediate action by the Council if that happened. Second, it proposes a joint *declaration* by the five avowed nuclear-weapon powers (who are also the five permanent members of the Security Council): Britain, China, France, Russia and the United States. In this declaration the nuclear five would (a) promise to refrain from using or threatening to use nuclear weapons first on a country that has forsworn such weapons, (b) agree to seek immediate Council action to provide assistance to such a country threatened or attacked first with nuclear weapons, and (c) reaffirm their right under the UN Charter to assist such a country individually as a matter of collective self-defense if the Council, because of a veto, is unable to act.[1]

Countries considering an agreement to refrain from acquiring nuclear weapons have in the past sought assurances of assistance in the event they were threatened with attack. U.S. alliance commitments to Germany, Italy and Japan seemed essential to gain their acceptance of non-nuclear-weapon status in the NPT during the late 1960s and early 1970s. In return for refraining from acquiring nuclear weapons, these three countries—each with advanced nuclear technology—relied upon a promise of assistance from a nuclear-weapon power (the United States) in the event of nuclear blackmail or attack by another nuclear-weapon power (the Soviet Union). Indeed, during the NPT negotiations Germany and Italy worked to change the duration specified in the U.S. and Soviet NPT drafts from "unlimited" to a shorter period, which they thought would be commensurate with the likely duration of the North Atlantic Treaty—NATO being their protection against possible nuclear attack.[2] These nations sought protection under the North Atlantic Treaty as long as they were obligated not to acquire nuclear weapons.

> *Countries considering an agreement to refrain from acquiring nuclear weapons have in the past sought assurances of assistance in the event they were threatened.*

Other forms of agreement for protecting the security of non-nuclear-weapon countries were considered during the NPT negotiation in the 1960s. The non-aligned countries that were considering accession to such a treaty asked the likely nuclear-weapon signers (the U.K., the Soviet Union, and the United States) to promise not to use or threaten to use nuclear weapons against a non-nuclear-weapon signer. This idea came to be known as a "negative security assurance." Some non-aligned countries also expressed their interest in being covered by an alliance-like "nuclear umbrella"—an assurance of assistance or protection by one or more nuclear-weapon states in the event they were threatened or attacked with nuclear weapons. This idea came to be called a "positive security assurance."[3]

The United States and the Soviet Union were unable to agree on language for negative security assurances in the context of the NPT.[4] Moreover, neither government wanted to expand its positive assurance alliance commitments to countries not already aligned with it—i.e. to hold its nuclear umbrella over all the non-nuclear-weapon countries that might join the NPT. The result was that the NPT itself contained no language on either form of security assurance. Instead, in 1968, a UN Security Council adopted a resolution, which recognized that "aggression with nuclear weapons or the threat of such aggression against a non-nuclear-weapon [s]tate would create a situation in which the Security Council, and above all its nuclear-weapon [s]tate permanent members, would have to act immediately in accordance with their obligations under the United Nations Charter" (Security Council Resolution 255). While negotiating the language of this resolution, Britain, the Soviet Union and the United States agreed to identical declarations stating their intention, as permanent members of the Security Council, "to seek immediate Security Council action to provide assistance, in accordance with the Charter, to any non-nuclear-weapon state party to the treaty on non-proliferation of nuclear weapons that is a victim of an act of aggression or an object of a threat of aggression in which nuclear weapons are used."[5]

Since then, the negative assurance issue has been raised repeatedly by Nigeria and others who support the NPT, but who wish to receive stronger security assurances for continuing to adhere to the NPT or for voting to extend the treaty in 1995.[6] They point to the unreasonableness of the U.S. demand that they, and others, forswear nuclear weapons indefinitely when the U.S. is unwilling even to promise not to use nuclear weapons against them.[7]

For over a decade, the multilateral Geneva Conference on Disarmament has attempted to find common ground on this issue. Nations supporting the NPT want assurances to be offered only to countries observing that treaty or a similar obligation such as a nuclear-free-zone treaty. Some non-NPT parties, including those that have not otherwise forsworn nuclear weapons (Pakistan, for instance), object to such a limitation. A variety of other points of view have been raised. The United States has been a reluctant negotiator in these talks, although it has not been entirely opposed to some form of negative assurance.[8] The U.S. has continued to oppose the promulgation of a promise not to use nuclear weapons against non-nuclear-weapon parties to the NPT, principally because it has been unwilling to relinquish the option to use nuclear weapons first—even against an adversary armed only with conventional weapons. In a last look at its non-proliferation policy, the Bush administration reviewed this question again just prior to the election, but it was not resolved.

All of the five avowed nuclear-weapon states have made at least qualified unilateral negative-assurance statements that are applicable globally, but each country's statement is different from the others.[9] The only statement all five have agreed on is in Additional Protocol II to the 1967 Latin American nuclear-free-zone treaty. In that protocol, the nuclear five agreed "not to use or threaten to use nuclear weapons against" parties to the treaty.[10] This promise was made to countries that by joining the Latin American treaty had agreed both to forswear nuclear weapons themselves and to prevent the deployment of nuclear weapons belonging to others on their territories. The NPT does not contain the second of these obligations. Indeed, the Soviet Union refused to agree to an NPT assurance of the Latin American treaty-sort for Germany, among others, since Germany had American nuclear weapons on its soil.[11]

In unilateral declarations not to use nuclear weapons against non-nuclear-weapon countries, Britain, France, and the United States qualified their promises not to use nuclear weapons against non-nuclear-weapon states because of NATO's decision to retain the option to use nuclear weapons first against an overwhelming conventional attack. The U.S. statement, made first in 1978 and repeated many times since, is as follows:

> The United States will not use nuclear weapons against any non-nuclear-weapon state party to the NPT or any comparable internationally binding commitment not to acquire nuclear explosive devices, *except in the case of an attack on the United States, its*

territories or armed forces, or its allies, by such a state allied to a nuclear-weapon state or associated with a nuclear-weapon state in carrying out or sustaining the attack.[12]

The Soviet Union stated in 1978 that it "will never use nuclear weapons against those States which renounce the production and acquisition of such weapons and do not have them on their territories." When signing the non-use provision for the Latin American nuclear-weapon-free zone, the Soviets issued a qualifying statement somewhat like the United States statement of 1978.[13]

With the end of bipolarity and the dissolution of the Soviet Union and the Warsaw Pact, the qualifications of the NATO countries and the Soviet Union seem outdated. NATO's post-Cold War strategy reflects "a reduced reliance on nuclear weapons," and the bulk of the U.S. nuclear weapons deployed on the territories of non-nuclear-weapon NATO allies, such as Germany, have been removed.[14] In the context of gaining a lengthy extension of the NPT in 1995, a further step toward a no-first-use strategy may now be possible.

With the end of the Cold War, an increasing number of analysts are prepared to say that the only purpose of nuclear weapons is to deter and respond to the first use of nuclear weapons by others. For example, the U.S. National Academy of Sciences' Committee on International Security and Arms Control has recommended that the United States and other nuclear-weapon states issue parallel declarations to this effect, and, in addition, promise not to use or threaten to use nuclear weapons against non-nuclear-weapon states.[15]

The Soviet Union stated in 1978 that it "will never use nuclear weapons against those States which renounce the production and acquisition of such weapons."

Some still argue that the United States must retain the ability to use nuclear weapons first against non-nuclear-weapon countries in regional conflicts,[16] but the United States did not use its nuclear capability in Vietnam or Korea when its forces were being beaten back. The chances that it would do so in the future are slim given the successes of its advanced-technology conventional forces in the Gulf War, and the stimulation to nuclear ambitions around the world that a U.S. first use of nuclear weapons—even a first-use strategy—could produce.

Moreover, the devastating loss of life that could follow implementation of such a strategy makes it morally and politically unacceptable.[17] Finally, it would work at cross purposes with the need to gain a broad-based political consensus to extend the NPT indefinitely. To convince other countries that they do not need nuclear weapons, the United States must demonstrate by its conduct that such weapons are not the most important protectors of its own security.

There have been other new developments relating to security assurances. China and France have become NPT members. Now all of the permanent members of the UN Security Council, those that have a veto, are also nuclear-weapon parties to the NPT. In 1968, France abstained from the Security Council positive-assurances resolution because it chose not to join the NPT. China was not then in the UN and assumed—with some justification—that it was the object of the 1968 resolution.

Kazakhstan and Ukraine initially demanded alliance-type security arrangements with the United States as part of the price for returning the nuclear weapons deployed on their territories when the Soviet Union collapsed. In 1992, Secretary of State Baker suggested that these governments refer to the 1968 Security Council resolution adopted when the NPT negotiation was completed. Baker noted that "the United States made a commitment [in 1968] to the effect generally that countries that subscribe to the NPT that were subjected to nuclear threats would have a friend in court, if you will, in the United States in the sense that we would bring the issue to the United Nations Security Council."[18] The presidents of Kazakhstan and Ukraine later both agreed to join the NPT as non-nuclear-weapon states.[19]

> *Kazakhstan and Ukraine fear a nuclear-armed Russia or China, each of whom could veto a UN Security Council action.*

The possible protection offered by a future Security Council action apparently had some credibility. However, Kazakhstan and Ukraine fear, whether reasonably or not, a nuclear-armed Russia or China, each of whom could veto a UN Security Council action. Though the Council has been operating effectively for several years on a wide variety of projects to keep the peace, to oversee settlement of regional disputes, and to counter aggression, a veto cannot be excluded. Thus, stronger positive-assurances by the Council, perhaps supported by the suggestion of individual or joint nuclear-weapon-state action if there were a veto and complemented by the addition of negative assurances from the nuclear-weapon states, would help to increase the credibility of the promise of protection for non-nuclear-weapon states.

In a September 1992 address to the UN General Assembly, President Bush suggested that the Security Council, including of course China and France, simply reaffirm the "assurances made at the time that the Nuclear Non-Proliferation Treaty was negotiated."[20] However, the time is ripe for more than that. Given China's hostility toward the 1968 resolution and its desire to participate in new arms control enterprises undertaken with the West, an exploration should be made of China's interest in a resolution and declaration against first use of nuclear weapons against countries foreswearing them. China has long advocated a no-first-use strategy with fewer qualifications than any of the other avowed nuclear-weapon states.[21] A new resolution could be made more attractive to China—as well as to the non-nuclear-weapon states whose support is so central to efforts to extend the NPT indefinitely—by including a prohibition on first use against all countries that have undertaken an obligation to abjure nuclear weapons. It is essential that China participate in this negotiation if the Security Council is to be used to confront nuclear blackmail against NPT parties not aligned with a nuclear-weapon country—as planned since 1968. China will inevitably be a part of the negotiation with the non-nuclear-weapon NPT parties to extend the treaty in 1995. What might make sense is a meeting of China and the other avowed nuclear-weapon countries in connection with Security Council business to plan for a new resolution, a five-power declaration and preparations for the 1995 NPT extension conference.

Attached as annexes are a draft UN Security Council resolution and a draft five-power declaration of the kind recommended here. The language on positive assurances strengthens the 1968 text by including a clearer statement that Security Council action would be taken, and that collective self-defense against a nuclear threat or attack would be possible in the event of a veto. However, the text would not constitute a legal promise of assistance or an alliance, and thus would not need to be promulgated in the form of a treaty.

The resolution and declaration would also be stronger than existing assurances, such as the one referred to be Secretary Baker, since they would contain negative security assurances. The language for these resolutions was drawn from the Latin American nuclear-free-zone treaty, but modified slightly to exclude protection for a non-nuclear-weapon NPT member that permitted a terrorist or another state to fire nuclear weapons from its territory. Finally, the resolution and declaration would be stronger not only because the record of cooperation in the Security Council over the last few years has been improving, but because all five permanent members would have participated in such a resolution.

ANNEX A
Draft UN Security Council Resolution on Security Assurances for States that Forswear Nuclear Weapons

The Security Council; *recalling* its Declaration of January 31, 1992 that the proliferation of nuclear and other weapons of mass destruction "constitutes a threat to international peace and security;" *recognizing* that nuclear weapons are the most devastating weapons of mass destruction; *welcoming* the observance of international obligations not to acquire nuclear weapons by over one hundred fifty (150) countries and the commitments by some of the countries that have nuclear weapons to cut their arsenals sharply; and *recognizing* the desires of many non-nuclear-weapon states for security arrangements to assure that there shall be no threat or use of nuclear weapons against them:

1. *Condemns* the threat or first use of nuclear weapons against any state observing an international obligation not to acquire nuclear weapons or other nuclear explosive devices,

2. *Recognizes* that such a threat or use of nuclear weapons would constitute a grave threat to international peace and security,

3. *Resolves* that such a threat or use of nuclear weapons would require the Council to act immediately in accordance with the Council's primary responsibility under the Charter for the maintenance of international peace and security,

4. *Welcomes* the Declaration by the permanent members that they will not threaten to use or use nuclear weapons first against any state observing an international obligation not acquire nuclear weapons or other nuclear explosive devices, and that, in accordance with the Charter, they will provide assistance to any such state that is the object of a threat or first use of nuclear weapons;

5. *Reaffirms* the inherent right, recognized by Article 51 of the Charter, of individual and collective self-defense if an armed attack occurs against a member of the United Nations, until the Security Council has taken measures necessary to maintain international peace and security.

ANNEX B
Draft Declaration by Permanent Members of the Security Council on Nuclear Security Assurances for States that Forswear Nuclear Weapons

The Permanent Members of the Council appreciate the concern of some states that continued renunciation of nuclear weapons could one day place them at a military disadvantage or make them vulnerable to nuclear blackmail.

The Permanent Members declare that they will not use or threaten to use nuclear weapons first against any state that is observing an international obligation not to acquire nuclear weapons or other nuclear explosive devices, hereafter called a "protected state."

The first-use of nuclear weapons, or the threat of such use against a protected state would require immediate action by the Council in exercise of its primary responsibility for the maintenance of international peace and security under Article 24 of the UN Charter.

As permanent members of the Security Council, the declarants promise to seek immediate Council action to provide assistance, in accordance with the Charter, to any protected state that is the object of a threat of use of nuclear weapons or the victim of a first-use.

The declarants reaffirm the inherent right, recognized under Article 51 of the Charter, of individual and collective self-defense if an armed attack occurs against a member of the United Nations, until the Security Council has taken measures necessary to maintain international peace and security. The declarants recognize that if the Council is convened to deal with a first-use of nuclear weapons against a protected state and the Council fails to take action, a right of individual and collective self-defense will exist.

Any state or sub-national group considering a first-use of nuclear weapons against a protected state is hereby warned that its actions will be countered by collective or individual responses taken in accordance with the UN Charter.

4.
Nuclear Testing and the Non-Proliferation Treaty

David A. Koplow

Introduction

Every lawyer acknowledges the importance of faithful adherence to binding legal obligations. Whether the instrument at bar is a commercial contract, a partnership agreement, or an international treaty, it is axiomatic that good faith compliance is essential: if we do not honor our commitments, then we cannot reasonably expect the other parties to fulfill their parts of the bargain, thereby casting doubt upon the entire system of fidelity to the rule of law.

In one critical area of international life, however, the United States has—for over a decade—flouted the key elements of the applicable law. Our government has reneged on repeated promises, frustrated the expectations of other nations and exposed the United States to damaging legal and political ramifications. This continued abandonment of solemn legal obligations threatens to undermine the pursuit of sound national policy in a crucial aspect of international relations: the non-proliferation of nuclear weapons.

This article examines the question of American fidelity to the international law of non-proliferation and nuclear weapons testing. It is organized into five main sections. The first describes the modern importance of non-proliferation and the key role played by the 1968 Non-Proliferation Treaty (NPT).[1] The second section focuses on nuclear weapons testing, the sequence of treaties and negotiations that have attempted incrementally to foreclose further explosions and the current American frustration of that effort. The third section probes the intersection of these two vital areas of international life, asking what obligations the United States has undertaken, in particular, what the disarmament provisions of Article VI of the NPT may require to abolish nuclear testing. The fourth section presents the "bottom line," marshalling the case for the proposition that the United States has committed a violation of the NPT by refusing to pursue a comprehensive nuclear test ban treaty. The fifth section then inquires into the legal and political remedies that might be available to other countries aggrieved by the United States breach, analyzing the juridical and diplomatic responses and their potential effects upon the United States and global security. Finally, a short conclusion attempts to place this controversy within the larger context of American efforts to establish a "new world order" based upon newfound respect for international law.

1. The Importance of Non-Proliferation and the NPT

With the Cold War behind us, many Americans are turning their attention to a host of regional and multilateral security issues that were long obscured by the persistent bipolar East-West confrontation. Foremost among these must be the dangers of the dissemination of weapons of mass destruction: nuclear, chemical, biological and other advanced weaponry, together with the aircraft or ballistic missiles that could deliver them. International violence today could spring from a variety of remote, troubled locales and quickly threaten United States interests and allies, engulfing us in increasingly expensive hostilities. As these more deadly armaments spread around the world, the planet becomes even more imperiled—the unsettling specter of Saddam Hussein, Moammar Gadhafi or others of their ilk armed with nuclear devices will pose some of the most challenging security dilemmas for American diplomacy into the next century.[2]

The Non-Proliferation Treaty is widely regarded as the cornerstone of the global effort to constrain those dangers and as such the NPT has become the most successful arms control regime in history, attracting more than one hundred sixty adherences, including the recent addition of some (such as China and South Africa) that had long been regarded as key "problem countries" for the non-proliferation regime.

The NPT is a starkly asymmetric arrangement. Under it, the so-called non-nuclear-weapon states (NNWS) agreed; 1) to refrain from receiving, manufacturing or otherwise acquiring nuclear explosive devices; and 2) to accept international safeguards implemented by the International Atomic Energy Agency (IAEA),[3] tolerating on-site inspection and other intrusions in order to verify compliance with the underlying non-armament provisions. In return, the nuclear-weapon states (NWS) undertook 1) not to assist or encourage any NNWS in acquiring nuclear weapons; 2) to share the myriad potential benefits of the atom for civilian nuclear power and engineering purposes; and 3) to proceed with further negotiations leading to nuclear disarmament.[4]

That last obligation—the commitment to additional measures of arms control—was a crucial component of the "basic bargain" of the NPT. The NNWS alleged that without it, the NPT would become an unacceptably "discriminatory" instrument, confining the NNWS to perpetual military inferiority as they eschewed a weapons capability that their NWS neighbors had apparently found to be essential to their own security. The NNWS accordingly insisted that the treaty combat not only "horizontal proliferation" (the spread of nuclear weapons to additional countries), but also "vertical proliferation" (the qualitative improvement of the nuclear arsenals of the NWS). A treaty that regulated only the former, without effective controls on the latter, would be politically intolerable and legally incomplete. Article VI of the NPT was therefore inserted into the treaty text at the insistence of the NNWS. It provides:

The commitment to additional measures of arms control was a crucial component of the "basic bargain" of the NPT.

> Each of the Parties to the Treaty undertakes to pursue negotiations *in good faith on effective measures relating to cessation of the nuclear arms race at an early date* and to nuclear disarmament, and on a treaty on general and complete disarmament under strict and effective international control. (Emphasis added.)

The principal mechanism for evaluating compliance with Article VI and the rest of the NPT has been the "Review Conferences," permitted every five years under Article VIII.3 of the treaty. To date, four such sessions have been convened and each has proven to be a raucous, contentious affair. On each occasion, the NNWS have complained bitterly about the poor NWS implementation record of Article VI, and—as we shall see below—the key component of this dissatisfaction has been the failure to conclude a comprehensive nuclear test ban treaty (CTBT). On two occasions—1980 and 1990—unrequited NNWS interest in a CTBT provoked such antagonism that the conference dissolved in anomie, preventing consensus upon any type of a final document or resolution.[5]

The 1995 conference will be of redoubled importance. Pursuant to Article X.2 of the NPT, that meeting will be the occasion where the parties determine—by simple majority vote—whether and how to extend the treaty beyond its initial twenty-five year duration.[6] The numerical superiority of the NNWS and their continued demands for enhanced compliance with the test ban obligations of Article VI will thus be a major factor in multilateral diplomacy in the coming years.[7]

2. The Importance of Nuclear Testing and Limitation

Since the dawn of the nuclear age, arms controllers have pursued efforts to halt the explosive testing of nuclear devices. A test ban accord was seen as crucial in circumscribing the qualitative improvement of the nuclear arsenals of the "have" countries as well as in arresting the spread of the destructive potential to the "have not" states.[8]

The first important limitation on nuclear testing—the first substantial post-World War II arms control accord of any sort—was the Limited Test Ban Treaty (LTBT) of 1963.[9] It prohibited nuclear explosions in the atmosphere, in outer space and under water—the three environments for which existing verification capabilities were deemed satisfactory—while permitting unrestricted testing underground.[10] The parties also noted in the LTBT preamble that they were still "seeking to achieve the discontinuance of all test explosions of nuclear weapons for all time and were determined to continue negotiations to this end."[11]

The next incremental advance in test bans was registered with the 1974 Threshold Test Ban Treaty (TTBT)[12] and its companion 1976 Peaceful Nuclear Explosions Treaty (PNET).[13] These were bilateral United States-Soviet Union accords, restricting the size of their underground explosions to one hundred fifty kilotons yield.[14] Again, the inability or unwillingness to conclude a CTBT was highlighted: Article I of the TTBT contains the obligation that "the Parties shall continue their negotiations with a view toward achieving a solution to the problem of the cessation of all underground nuclear weapon tests."

Through it all, a CTBT has eluded the negotiators. The United States, Soviet Union and United Kingdom wrestled through several rounds of negotiations from 1977 through 1980, reaching a substantial amount of agreement on a draft treaty text, but they were unable to conclude a complete accord.[15] The subject of additional testing limitations has remained under active consideration in both the United Nations General Assembly (UNGA) and the Conference on Disarmament (the primary forum for multilateral disarmament negotiations). The voting on the now-annual UNGA resolution in support of prompt CTBT negotiation has revealed approximately one hundred twenty countries in favor and typically only the United States and United Kingdom opposed.[16]

The Reagan and Bush administrations, in fact, have been resolute opponents of several different types of efforts to further constrain nuclear weapons testing. In 1981, President Reagan reversed the prior United States policy dating back to the Eisenhower administration and suspended the CTBT negotiations, turning attention instead to the laborious negotiation of additional verification protocols to augment the provisions of the TTBT and PNET.[17] In 1986, he promised the Congress that negotiations on additional testing limitations would commence "immediately" after the entry into force of those protocols,[18] but President Bush has backed away from that commitment.[19] Kenneth Adelman, Director of the United States Arms Control and Disarmament Agency blithely declared in 1987 that a CTBT would be pursued only "way, way, way down the road . . . when

Since the dawn of the nuclear age, arms controllers have pursued efforts to halt the explosive testing of nuclear devices.

there's peace on earth and good will towards men."[20] In 1990, his successor as ACDA Director, Ronald F. Lehman II, testified to the Senate Armed Services Committee that test ban negotiations would be resumed in a matter of "months, not years"[21]—yet no talks resumed. In fact, in 1991 when prodding by NNWS generated an "Amendment Conference" of LTBT parties to consider altering that instrument to convert it into a CTBT, the United States again blocked all efforts, resisting even the proposal to sustain CTBT as a leading subject of ongoing international deliberations.[22]

The Soviet Union, and subsequently Russia, on the other hand, have been consistent champions of a CTBT. Mikhail Gorbachev featured the test ban prominently on his international agenda and he and Boris Yeltsin have undertaken a series of unilateral moratoria, suspending all nuclear explosions and calling for American reciprocity. The international "box score" of nuclear explosions reveals that the United States has conducted 936 tests since 1945, the Soviet Union 715, France 192, the United Kingdom 44, China 36, and India 1. In the more recent past, the totals for 1990 and 1991 were: United States 15, Soviet Union/Russia 1, France 12, United Kingdom 2, China 2, and India 0.[23]

3. The Relationship Between NPT and CTBT

The text of Article VI of the NPT does not refer explicitly to a CTBT or to any other particular "effective measure" of nuclear arms control. However, the treaty's preamble (widely regarded as shedding important light upon the negotiators' "object and purpose" in concluding the accord) does "recall" the LTBT and the parties' determination to continue negotiations toward a total cessation of testing—and CTBT is the only specific arms control measure identified as such in the preamble.[24]

Under the Vienna Convention on the Law of Treaties,[25] a hierarchy of legal authorities is established to aid in the interpretation of an ambiguous document. Context, contemporaneous agreements, subsequent agreements, subsequent practice and the negotiating history of the accord may all assist in plumbing the intention behind the language of the document.[26]

In the case of the NPT, the 1965-68 political milieu establishes not only that Article VI was absolutely fundamental to the conclusion of a mutually acceptable treaty, but also that CTBT was the foremost "effective measure" that the parties contemplated for prompt effectuation. A reading of the negotiating history demonstrates that the NNWS in the early and middle 1960s were quite concerned about the spread of nuclear weaponry; they properly saw themselves as imperiled and a multilateral treaty as a salutary development. At the same time, they were unwilling to guarantee the NWS a privileged place forever. If the NNWS were to forego nuclear weapons, then the NWS should undertake comparable, offsetting disarmament obligations, too. The NPT was thus seen as only a partial, interim measure, to "freeze" the status quo and avoid further deterioration through additional proliferation. The true, long-term objective was the complete abolition of all nuclear weapons by all states equally.[27]

The negotiating parties acknowledged that several different types of "effective measures" could play a valuable role in reversing the ongoing spiral of the nuclear arms race: limitations upon strategic offensive weapons (which ultimately gave rise to the SALT negotiations in 1969, followed by START in the 1980s), security assurances or non-use declarations, a "cut-off" of production of fissionable materials and other devices were suggested and endorsed. However, the leading issue of the day was CTBT—it had long been the key desideratum of arms controllers, attaining a unique degree of support and international public appeal. CTBT was repeatedly highlighted as the key ingredient in the global security structure that the NPT was attempting to promote. Delegates from Sweden, Germany, India, Japan, Nigeria and elsewhere all featured it in their addresses to the negotiating body.[28]

CTBT was repeatedly highlighted as the key ingredient in the global security structure that the NPT was attempting to promote.

The United States, too, endorsed CTBT during the negotiations, and President Johnson, Secretary of State Rusk, and U.S. Ambassador to the UN Arthur Goldberg all affirmed that CTBT was a primary American negotiating objective for the near term, to be taken up promptly upon the conclusion of the NPT.[29] To be sure, the United States was cautious about the anticipated Soviet behavior during any CTBT negotiations—Americans were worried that the Soviets might, as they had during the LTBT negotiations in 1963, publicly endorse a CTBT, but privately resist the essential verification arrangements. The United States thus campaigned to keep out of Article VI any direct reference to CTBT in particular, to avoid entrenching a particular timetable for the negotiations or any mandatory sequence of arms control initiatives to be developed.[30]

Likewise, the "subsequent practice" of NPT parties, especially as reflected in the statements issued at the four quinquennial review conferences, establishes the primacy of CTBT. As early as the 1975 conference, the NNWS were complaining about the NWS failure to move more promptly on test ban limitations. The TTBT was dismissed as an inadequate substitute because it simply confirmed the superpowers' testing plans and practices without significantly restricting them.[31] By the 1980 assembly—the only occasion during which CTBT negotiations were even technically underway[32]—the NNWS led by Mexico demanded faster action on a test ban and when the United States resisted the inclusion of such strong language into the conference's final report, the entire document was discarded in disarray.[33]

The next two review conferences—held in the face of Reagan/Bush antipathy to test bans—were just as acrimonious. The NNWS were urging greater fealty to Article VI and the United States was insisting that other measures of arms control (such as limitations upon intermediate-range nuclear forces and upon conventional forces in Europe) were adequate to discharge the general arms control obligations of Article VI, even without a test ban.[34]

In rereading the documents from this period—the run-up to the 1968 negotiations, the declarations of the various review conferences and the other surrounding materials—two impressions predominate. First, for the NNWS, CTBT remains the key item of "old business." These nations are arguing not merely that a test ban would be a sound development for international peace and stability, and not merely that it would help redress an imbalance in global military power. They are arguing, in addition, that a CTBT is *already required* by Article VI—that the United States agreed to this tradeoff in 1968, that the rest of the world has relied in vain upon the assurance that a CTBT would be a priority negotiating objective and that the entire scheme of the NPT relies upon pursuit of test ban as the key (not the sole, but the single most important) effective measure for reversing the nuclear arms race.

The second clear impression is that the United States has dramatically changed its interpretation of Article VI over the years. In 1969, in presenting a proposed disarmament agenda for the consideration of multilateral negotiators, the United States and the Soviet Union jointly listed CTBT first among the possible avenues.[35] This document reflected the consistent attitude of the United States and the Soviet Union that a CTBT was a logical international priority to be taken up when the NPT was concluded. By 1985, however, the United States' approach had altered: CTBT was no longer obligatory, urgent, or even desirable. Since a test ban treaty would interfere with the projected buildup of United States military capacity, it could not be implemented; so long as the United States depended upon nuclear weapons for deterrence, testing would be required.[36] Only in some far-off nirvana, where nuclear (and other) weapons have essentially disappeared and where all possible verification reservations have been erased, would CTBT negotiations again become thinkable.[37]

This obstruction of test bans has recently become even more problematic. Russia and France have both suspended all their testing (although Boris Yeltsin has made preparations to resume the explosions if the United States does not reciprocate.) The projected nuclear re-armament of America has been replaced in the post-Cold War era with a race to disarm, rendering major parts of the existing arsenal suddenly obsolete and redundant. The large financial cost of detonating a nuclear weapon has already cut in half the size of the annual American testing program. The United States government, moreover, has already ceased the production of nuclear bomb-grade fissionable materials and has unilaterally canceled plans for building any additional types of nuclear devices.

In July 1992, the Bush administration further announced that it would limit the future testing program to no more than six explosions per year, with no more than three to be larger than thirty-five kilotons. Furthermore, all the tests would be dedicated to assessing the safety and reliability of existing weapons designs already in the stockpile, rather than to the development of new types of weapons.[38] Experts criticized this continuing testing strategy as unnecessary—only a handful of explosions would now be needed under any circumstances for safety and reliability purposes.[39]

Most dramatically, the Congress is now in the process of debating legislation that would, in one way or another, cut off further American nuclear testing so long as Russia reciprocates.[40] The United States House of Representatives has repeatedly passed resolutions of support for renewal of CTBT negotiations and a moratorium on United States testing. In 1992, binding legislation again passed the House and, for the first time, passed the Senate too. Further legislative action, including full House-Senate Conference Committee workup, is anticipated during the fall. Nevertheless, the Bush administration has threatened to veto any such enactment and has adamantly resisted progress on test bans. As a result, no international negotiations toward a CTBT have occurred since 1980.

4. Has the United States Violated Article VI?

Article VI of the NPT is hardly a model of drafting clarity and elegance. It is easier, therefore, to state with conviction what the treaty does *not* require. First, the NPT does not obligate the United States or any other country to conclude a CTBT by any particular date. It does not even mandate a precise timetable for the initiation of the negotiations, or require that a CTBT be nudged ahead of all other items on the international disarmament agenda. Furthermore, Article VI does not compel the United States or any other country to make any specific concessions in the international bargaining, to abandon any positions related to verification or other questions, or to accept any particular compromises offered by other states.

At the same time, Article VI is not a dead letter. It does require that the United States negotiate in "good faith" in pursuit of "effective measures" of nuclear arms reduction. The contemporaneous context and subsequent practice make clear that of all the possible "effective measures" that the parties had in contemplation in 1968, CTBT was the most important and urgent. This continued to be the view of the international community from 1968 onward, with the exception of the United States which essentially abandoned comprehensive test ban negotiations after 1980.

For many people, the phrase "good faith" may seem hopelessly amorphous as guidance for negotiations. Lawyers, however, who encounter the term and grapple with its meaning in a variety of domestic and international legal contexts, know that a vague and imprecise obligation is not necessarily the same as a void one and that a commitment to comport oneself in a particular fashion can have some teeth.[41]

In domestic United States labor-management bargaining, for example, the National Labor Relations Act requires that the two sides negotiate "in good faith" on a variety of workplace issues.[42] Although this standard, like the NPT, is delphic, courts and commentators have not hesitated to construe it and to import additional meaning. The sides must, for example, demonstrate a "sincere desire to reach an agreement."[43] They are not required to change any particular positions or to accept specific offers on specified issues—hard, positional bargaining is accepted as fully legitimate. However, they must come to the bargaining table, they must make some effort to define mutually acceptable alternatives, and they must, in the overall conduct of their approach to the deliberations, demonstrate a commitment to the effort to solve the problems.[44]

International law contains cognate principles. The Vienna Convention mandates "good faith" in interpreting and implementing international agreements,[45] and the International Court of Justice (ICJ) has frequently had the occasion to construe that term, treating it as a meaningful, albeit obscure, point of law.[46] Both the ICJ and its predecessor, the Permanent Court of International Justice, have ruled that a mandate for good faith international negotiation

> *In other arms control contexts, the U.S. has long championed a hard-nosed approach to good faith deliberations.*

requires each party to approach the bargaining with an open mind, sincerely attempting to develop viable solutions, not simply insisting upon having its own way.[47]

In other arms control contexts, the United States has long championed a hard-nosed approach to good faith deliberations. Whether the issue was the poor Soviet record of withholding information necessary to clarify the status of the Krasnoyarsk radar[48] or the true nature of the outbreak of anthrax at Sverdlovsk,[49] the United States insisted upon a high level of active cooperation and asserted that the failure to be more forthcoming in the effort to resolve these types of issues "calls into question" the other party's *bona fides* on the entire range of arms control controversies.[50]

The most interesting response the United States government might assert to ward off a finding of breach would be to attempt to invoke the international law doctrine of "changed circumstances," also known as *rebus sic stantibus*. Analogous to domestic contract law principles, in which obligations may sometimes be avoided if the fundamental basis of the agreement has been altered by exogenous circumstances, *rebus sic stantibus* has never been a favored doctrine under international law. The United States, in particular, has rarely been hospitable to assertions of changed circumstances, especially in the context of arms control accords, and *rebus sic stantibus* has never been successfully invoked in ICJ or other international litigation.[51]

Nevertheless, the standards of the Vienna Convention might seem to make it applicable here.[52] The startling breakthroughs across the arms control board were manifestly "not foreseen" by the NPT negotiators and those changes have indeed "radically transformed" the "essential basis" of the international security relationships that prevailed in 1968.

However, these alterations are not at all the type of modifications that should grant the United States unilateral freedom to wiggle off the Article VI hook. First, the ending of the Cold War, while not exactly "foreseen" by the NPT drafters, was precisely the type of improvement in international relations that they were *attempting* to facilitate. Second, the recent and ongoing changes have, in the main, made a CTBT *more* attractive, valuable and feasible—they have eliminated some of the potential hurdles (such as the traditional Soviet paranoia in resisting intrusive verification) that had previously stood in the way of a test ban. Finally, the arms control progress in recent years has not in any way ameliorated the fundamental point that Article VI was addressing: the division of the world into NNWS and NWS was intended to be a temporary expedient, not perpetuated forever—and CTBT was a principle vehicle for terminating that type of discrimination.

In short, what has "changed" since 1968-1970 is not the objective "circumstances" of the NPT. Instead, the United States has simply "changed its mind" about the wisdom of concluding a comprehensive nuclear test ban—and that type of post-agreement remorse is not legally protected.[53]

5. Remedies for Violation of the NPT and TTBT

If the United States has, indeed, violated the disarmament provisions of Article VI of the NPT and Article I of the TTBT, what can the rest of the world do about it? Clearly, the power realities of the planet would not allow other countries physically to enforce their will against the sole remaining superpower—in today's international structure, no one could compel a CTBT upon an unwilling American behemoth. There are nonetheless three types of damaging "remedies" available under international law and practice.

First, the aggrieved nations could invoke the remedial provisions of the Vienna Convention.[54] There, a "material breach" is defined as either a repudiation or a violation of an essential provision of the treaty. Arguably, the American statements of intention not to engage in CTBT negotiations and the failure in fact to submit to negotiations satisfy both criteria. An extended period of notification and mandatory recourse to various mechanisms for the pacific settlement of disputes are then invoked, under the auspices of the United Nations, the ICJ and other institutions.

Under international law, one or more countries aggrieved by another state's material breach of a multilateral treaty are authorized to "suspend the operation of the treaty in whole or in part or to terminate it."[55] In the case of the NPT, an innocent party might therefore cite the United States' violation of Article VI as a justification for its own decision to cease cooperation with IAEA inspectors, to withdraw selected facilities from the application of safeguards, or, in the extreme, to announce that it was then undertaking a national program of pursuit of the nuclear weapons option.[56]

A second possible approach—both more serious and more likely—for vindicating legal rights trammeled by the American departure from Article VI could arise in the context of the 1995 NPT extension conference.[57] There, parties agitated by American hostility toward a

CTBT might respond by refusing to consent to any substantial pro-longation of the treaty. They might, for example, agree to only a short, fixed additional duration, with the understanding that the treaty could be resurrected, in some fashion only by the parallel conclusion of a CTBT.[58] This ploy would, doubtless, be resisted by NPT stalwarts, who would deride it as "throwing the NPT baby out with the CTBT bathwater," but it may have considerable political appeal to NNWS countries feeling "taken" by the NWS' unfulfilled promises on Article VI.

Third, the NNWS might pursue a more general, less cataclysmic approach of continuing to confront the United States on the CTBT issue at every diplomatic opportunity, isolating the American government even from its traditional allies and attempting to turn up the political heat at every occasion. The NNWS could continue their annual efforts inside the United Nations and the Conference on Disarmament. They could attempt to reconvene the LTBT amendment conference. They could seek to assemble a similar amendment conference for the NPT itself.[59] They could solicit an "advisory opinion" on the question from the ICJ.[60] None of these actions, by itself, could bring the United States to capitulate on the CTBT issue, but together they might help persuade a calculating American leadership that continued opposition to test ban progress was no longer worth the cost, especially in light of the rather dubious alleged gains from sustaining a reduced testing program of modest scope.[61]

Conclusion

In the long run, violations of international law are usually not free. The United States, like other, less powerful countries, will eventually be forced to pay some sort of price for its continued transgression of the test ban obligations of NPT Article VI and TTBT Article I. At the very least, the United States government will be exposed as hypocritical, giving speeches advocating the creation of a "new world order" based upon fealty to the rule of international law when that serves our purposes, but simultaneously sustaining an important violation of solemn international agreements.

In fact, the United States has the greatest interest in the establishment and promotion of the system of international law. The United

States is the foremost maker of treaties and we stand to lose the most when that mechanism of international communication and exchange is degraded. We have the greatest stake in the continuity of international relations and we should insist that all states pay close heed   to the cooperative demands of the international community. The model of a powerful rogue nation, blithely thumbing its nose at the international community and insisting upon its right to violate its international agreements and exploit alleged loopholes for unilateral advantage is hardly the precedent we should seek to entrench.

We should all hope that the NPT survives the 1995 conference and continues to flourish as the central element in the global non-proliferation effort—pursuing that avenue for international peace and stability will provide the greatest challenges to our creativity and persistence into the next century. The key next move for the United States in that vein is to reverse the current antipathy toward a comprehensive nuclear test ban treaty and live up to our Article VI obligations to negotiate and help bring into force a CTBT without further delay.

The 1968 Treaty on the Non-Proliferation of Nuclear Weapons

Preamble

The States concluding this Treaty, hereinafter referred to as the "Parties to the Treaty",

Considering the devastation that would be visited upon all mankind by a nuclear war and the consequent need to make every effort to avert the danger of such a war and to take measures to safeguard the security of peoples,

Believing that the proliferation of nuclear weapons would seriously enhance the danger of nuclear war,

In conformity with resolutions of the United Nations General Assembly calling for the conclusion of an agreement on the prevention of wider dissemination of nuclear weapons,

Undertaking to cooperate in facilitating the application of International Atomic Energy Agency safeguards on peaceful nuclear activities,

Expressing their support for research, development and other efforts to further the application, within the framework of the International

Atomic Energy Agency safeguards system, of the principle of safe-guarding effectively the flow of source and special fissionable materials by use of instruments and other techniques at certain strategic points,

Affirming the principle that the benefits of peaceful applications of nuclear technology, including any technological by-products which may be derived by nuclear-weapon States from the development of nuclear explosive devices, should be available for peaceful purposes to all Parties of the Treaty, whether nuclear-weapon or non-nuclear-weapon States,

Convinced that, in furtherance of this principle, all Parties to the Treaty are entitled to participate in the fullest possible exchange of scientific information for, and to contribute alone or in cooperation with other States to, the further development of the applications of atomic energy for peaceful purposes,

Declaring their intention to achieve at the earliest possible date the cessation of the nuclear arms race and to undertake effective measures in the directions of nuclear disarmament,

Urging the cooperations of all States in the attainment of this objective,

Recalling the determination expressed by the Parties to the 1963 Treaty banning nuclear weapon tests in the atmosphere, in outer space and under water in its Preamble to seek to achieve the discontinuance of all test explosions of nuclear weapons for all time and to continue negotiations to this end,

Desiring to further the easing of international tension and the strengthening of trust between States in order to facilitate the cessation of the manufacture of nuclear weapons, the liquidation of all their existing stockpiles, and the elimination from national arsenals of nuclear weapons and the means of their delivery pursuant to a treaty on general and complete disarmament under strict and effective international control,

Recalling that, in accordance with the Charter of the United Nations, States must refrain in their international relations from the threat or use of force against the territorial integrity or political independence of any State, or in any other manner inconsistent with the Purposes of the United Nations, and that the establishment and maintenance of international peace and security are to be promoted with the least diversion for armaments of the world's human and economic resources,

Have agreed as follows:

Article I

Each nuclear-weapon State Party to the Treaty undertakes not to transfer to any recipient whatsoever nuclear weapons or other nuclear explosive devices or control over such weapons or explosive devices directly, or indirectly; and not in any way to otherwise acquire nuclear weapons or other nuclear explosive devices, or control over such weapons or explosive devices.

Article II

Each non-nuclear-weapon State Party to the Treaty undertakes not to receive the transfer from any transferor whatsoever of nuclear weapons or other nuclear explosive devices or of control over such weapons or explosive devices directly, or indirectly; not to manufacture or otherwise acquire nuclear weapons or other nuclear explosive devices; and not to seek or receive any assistance in the manufacture of nuclear weapons or other nuclear explosive devices.

Article III

1. Each non-nuclear-weapon State Party to the Treaty undertakes to accept safeguards, as set forth in an agreement to be negotiated and concluded with the International Atomic Energy Agency in accordance with the Statute of the International Atomic Energy Agency and the Agency's safeguards system, for the exclusive purpose of verification of the fulfillment of its obligations assumed under this Treaty with a view to preventing diversion of nuclear energy from peaceful uses to nuclear weapons of other nuclear explosive devices. Procedures for the safeguards required by this article shall by followed with respect to source or special fissionable material whether

it is being produced, processed or used in any principal nuclear facility or is outside any such facility. The safeguards required by this article shall be applied to all source or special fissionable material in all peaceful nuclear activities within the territory of such State, under its jurisdiction, or carried out under its control anywhere.

2. Each State Party to the Treaty undertakes not to provide: (a) source or special fissionable material, or (b) equipment or material especially designed or prepared for the processing, use or production of special fissionable material, to any non-nuclear-weapon State for peaceful purposes, unless the source of special fissionable material shall be subject to the safeguards required by this Article.

3. The safeguards required by this Article shall be implemented in a manner designed to comply with Article IV of this Treaty, and to avoid hampering the economic or technological development of the Parties or international cooperation in the field of peaceful nuclear activities, including the international exchange of nuclear material and equipment for the processing, use or production of nuclear material for peaceful purposes in accordance with the provisions of this article and the principle of safeguarding set forth in the Preamble of the Treaty.

4. Non-nuclear-weapon States Party to the Treaty shall conclude agreements with the International Atomic Energy Agency to meet the requirements of this Article either individually or together with other States in accordance with the Statute of the International Atomic Energy Agency. Negotiation of such agreements shall commence within 180 days from the original entry into force of this Treaty. For States depositing their instruments of ratification of accession after the 180-day period, negotiation of such agreements shall commence not later than the date of such deposit. Such agreements shall enter into force not later than eighteen months after the date of initiation of negotiations.

Article IV

1. Nothing in this Treaty shall by interpreted as affecting the inalienable right of all the Parties to the Treaty to develop research, production and use of nuclear energy for peaceful purposes without discrimination and in conformity with Articles I and II of this Treaty.

2. All the Parties to the Treaty undertake to facilitate, and have the right to participate in, the fullest possible exchange of equipment, materials and scientific and technological information for the peaceful uses of nuclear energy. Parties to the Treaty in a position to do so shall also cooperate in contributing alone or together with other States or international organizations to the further development of the applications of nuclear energy for peaceful purposes, especially in the territories of non-nuclear-weapon States Party to the Treaty, with due consideration for the needs of the developing areas of the World.

Article V

Each party to the Treaty undertakes to take appropriate measures to ensure that, in accordance with this Treaty, under appropriate international observation and through appropriate international procedures, potential benefits from any peaceful applications of nuclear explosions will be made available to non-nuclear-weapon States Party to the Treaty on a nondiscriminatory basis and that the charge to such Parties for the explosive devices used will be as low as possible and exclude any charge for research and development. Non-nuclear-weapon States Party to the Treaty shall be able to obtain such benefits, pursuant to a special international agreement or agreements, through an appropriate international body with adequate representation of non-nuclear-weapon States. Negotiations on this subject shall commence as soon as possible after the Treaty enters into force. Non-nuclear-weapon States Party to the Treaty so desiring may also obtain such benefits pursuant to bilateral agreements.

Article VI

Each of the Parties to the Treaty undertakes to pursue negotiations in good faith on effective measures relating to cessation of the nuclear arms race at an early date and to nuclear disarmament, and on a treaty on general and complete disarmament under strict and effective international control.

Article VII

Nothing in this Treaty affects the right of any group of States to conclude regional treaties in order to assure the total absence of nuclear weapons in their respective territories.

Article VIII

1. Any Party to the Treaty may propose amendments to this Treaty. The text of any proposed amendment shall be submitted to the Depositary Governments which shall circulate it to all Parties to the Treaty. Thereupon, if requested to do so by one-third or more of the Parties to the Treaty, the Depositary Governments shall convene a conference, to which they shall invite all the Parties to the Treaty, to consider such an amendment.

2. Any amendment to the Treaty must be approved by a majority of the votes of all the Parties to the Treaty, including the votes of all nuclear-weapons States Party to the Treaty and all other Parties which, on the date the amendment is circulated, are members of the Board of Governors of the International Atomic Energy Agency. The amendment shall enter into force for each Party that deposits its instrument of ratification of the amendment upon the deposit of such instruments of ratification by a majority of all the Parties, including the instruments of ratification of all nuclear-weapons States Party to the Treaty and all other Parties which, on the date the amendment is circulated, are members of the Board of Governors of the International Atomic Energy Agency. Thereafter, it shall enter into force for any other Party upon the deposit of its instrument of ratification of the amendment.

3. Five years after the entry into force of this Treaty, a conference of Parties to the Treaty shall be held in Geneva, Switzerland, in order to review the operation of this Treaty with a view to assuring that the purposes of the Preamble and the provisions of the Treaty are being realized. At intervals of five years thereafter, a majority of the Parties to the Treaty may obtain, by submitting a proposal to this effect to the Depositary Governments, the convening of further conferences with the same objective of reviewing the operation of the Treaty.

Article IX

1. This Treaty shall be open to all States for signature. Any State which does not sign the Treaty before its entry into force in accordance with paragraph 3 of this Article may accede to it at any time.

2. This Treaty shall be subject to ratification by signatory States. Instruments of ratification and instruments of accession shall be deposited with the Governments of the United States of America, the United Kingdom of Great Britain and Northern Ireland and the Union of Soviet Socialist Republics, which are hereby designated the Depositary Governments.

3. This Treaty shall enter into force after its ratification by the State, the Governments of which are designated Depositaries of the Treaty, and forty other States signatory to this Treaty and the deposit of their instruments of ratification. For the purposes of this Treaty, a nuclear-weapon State is one which has manufactured and exploded a nuclear weapon or other nuclear explosive device prior to January 1, 1967.

4. For States whose instruments of ratification or accession are deposited subsequent to the entry into force of this Treaty, it shall enter into force on the date of the deposit of their instruments of ratification or accession.

5. The Depositary Governments shall promptly inform all signatory and acceding States of the date of each signature, the date of deposit of each instrument of ratification or of accession, the date of the entry into force of this Treaty, and the date of receipt of any requests for convening a conference or other notices.

6. This Treaty shall be registered by the Depositary Governments pursuant to Article 102 of the Charter of the United Nations.

Article X

1. Each Party shall in exercising its national sovereignty have the right to withdraw from the Treaty if it decides that extraordinary events, related to the subject matter of this Treaty, have jeopardized the supreme interests of its country. It shall give notice of such

withdrawal to all other Parties to the Treaty and to the United Nations Security Council three months in advance. Such notice shall include a statement of the extraordinary events it regards as having jeopardized its supreme interests.

2. Twenty-five years after the entry into force of the Treaty, a conference shall by convened to decide whether the Treaty shall continue in force indefinitely, or shall be extended for an additional fixed period or periods. This decision shall be taken by a majority of the Parties to the Treaty.

Article XI

This Treaty, the English, Russian, French, Spanish and Chinese texts of which are equally authentic, shall be deposited in the archives of the Depositary Governments. Duly certified copies of this Treaty shall be transmitted by the Depositary Governments to the Governments of the of the Signatory and acceding States.

Signatories and Parties to the NPT

as of April 1, 1994

Country	Date of Signature	Date of Deposit of Ratification	Date of Deposit of Accession (A) or Succession (S)
Afghanistan*	7/1/68	2/4/70	
Albania**			9/12/90(A)
Antigua & Barbuda			6/17/85(S)
Armenia			7/15/93(A)
Australia*	2/27/70	1/23/73	
Austria*	7/1/68	6/27/69	
Azerbaijan			9/22/92(A)
Bahamas, The			8/11/76(S)
Bahrain			11/3/88(A)
Bangladesh*			8/31/79(A)
Barbados	7/1/68	2/21/80	
Belarus			7/22/93(A)

Dates given are the earliest dates on which a country signed the Treaty or deposited its instrument of ratification or accession—whether in Washington, London or Moscow. In the case of a country that was a dependent territory which became a party through succession, the date given is the date on which the country gave notice that it would continue to be bound by the terms of the Treaty.

* Entries with asterisk have NPT safeguards agreements that have entered into force as of 10/31/92, not 4/1/94.

Country	Date of Signature	Date of Deposit of Ratification	Date of Deposit of Accession (A) or Succession (S)
Belgium*	8/20/68	5/2/75	
Belize			8/9/85 (S)
Benin	7/1/68	10/31/72	
Bhutan*			5/23/85 (A)
Bolivia	7/1/68	5/26/70	
Botswana	7/1/68	4/28/69	
Brunei*			3/26/85 (A)
Bulgaria*	7/1/68	9/5/69	
Burkina Faso	11/25/68	3/3/70	
Burundi			3/19/71 (A)
Cambodia			6/2/72 (A)
Cameroon	7/17/68	1/8/69	
Canada*	7/23/68	1/8/69	
Cape Verde			10/24/79 (A)
Central African Republic			10/25/70 (A)
Chad	7/1/68	3/10/71	
China			3/9/92 (A)
Colombia**	7/1/68	4/8/86	
Congo			10/23/78 (A)
Costa Rica*	7/1/68	3/3/70	
Cote d'Ivoire*	7/1/68	3/6/73	
Croatia			6/29/92 (S)
Cyprus*	7/1/68	2/10/70	
Czech Republic*			1/1/93 (S)
Denmark*	7/1/68	1/3/69	
Dominica			8/10/84 (S)
Dominican Republic*	7/1/68	7/24/71	
Ecuador*	7/9/68	3/7/69	
Egypt*	7/1/68	2/26/81 [1]	
El Salvador*	7/1/68	7/11/72	
Equatorial Guinea			11/1/84 (A)
Estonia			1/7/92 (A)
Ethiopia*	9/5/68	2/5/70	
Fiji*			7/14/72 (S)
Finland*	7/1/68	2/5/69	

** Non-NPT, full-scope safeguards agreement in force.

[1] With Statement.

Country	Date of Signature	Date of Deposit of Ratification	Date of Deposit of Accession (A) or Succession (S)
France			8/3/92(A)
Gabon			2/19/74(A)
Gambia,* The	9/4/68	5/12/75	
Georgia			3/7/94(A)
Germany,* Fed Rep of	11/28/69	5/2/75 [1,2]	
Ghana*	7/1/68	5/4/70	
Greece*	7/1/68	3/11/70	
Grenada			9/2/75(S)
Guatemala*	7/26/68	9/22/70	
Guinea			4/29/85(A)
Guinea-Basau			8/20/76(S)
Guyana			10/19/93(A)
Haiti	7/1/68	6/2/70	
Holy See*			2/25/71(A) [1]
Honduras*	7/1/68	5/16/73	
Hungary*, Rep of	7/1/68	5/27/69	
Iceland*	7/1/68	7/18/69	
Indonesia*	3/2/70	7/12/79 [1]	
Iran*	7/1/68	2/2/70	
Iraq*	7/1/68	10/29/69	
Ireland*	7/1/68	7/1/68	
Italy*	1/28/69	5/2/75 [1]	
Jamaica*	4/14/69	3/5/70	
Japan*	2/3/70	6/8/75 [1]	
Jordan*	7/10/68	2/11/70	
Kazakhstan			2/14/94(A)
Kenya	7/1/68	6/11/70	
Kiribati*			4/18/85(S)
Korea, Dem People's Rep of			12/12/85(A)
Korea*, Rep of	7/1/68	4/23/75	
Kuwait	8/15/68	11/17/89	
Laos	7/1/68	2/20/70	
Latvia			1/31/92(A)
Lebanon*	7/1/68	7/15/70	
Lesotho*	7/9/68	5/20/70	

---

[2] The former German Democratic Republic, which united with the Federal Republic of Germany on 10/3/90, had signed the NPT on 7/1/68 and deposited its instrument of ratification on 10/31/69.

Country	Date of Signature	Date of Deposit of Ratification	Date of Deposit of Accession (A) or Succession (S)
Liberia	7/1/68	3/5/70	
Libya*	7/18/68	5/26/75	
Liechtenstein*			4/20/78(A) [1]
Lithuania			9/23/91(A)
Luxembourg*	8/14/68	5/2/75	
Madagascar*	8/22/68	10/8/70	
Malawi*			2/18/86(S)
Malaysia*	7/1/68	3/5/70	
Maldives*	9/11/68	4/7/70	
Mali	7/14/69	2/10/70	
Malta*	4/17/69	2/6/70	
Mauritania			10/23/93(A)
Maurtius*	7/1/68	4/8/69	
Mexico*	7/26/68	1/21/69 [1]	
Mongolia*	7/1/68	5/14/69	
Morocco*	7/1/68	11/27/70	
Mozambique			9/4/90(A)
Myanmar (Burma)			12/2/92(A)
Namibia			10/2/92(A)
Nauru*			6/7/82(A)
Nepal*	7/1/68	1/5/70	
Netherlands*	8/20/68	5/2/75 [3]	
New Zealand*	7/1/68	9/10/69	
Nicaragua*	7/1/68	3/6/73	
Niger			10/9/92(A)
Nigeria*	7/1/68	9/27/68	
Norway*	7/1/68	2/5/69	
Panama	7/1/68	1/13/77	
Papua New Guinea*			1/13/82(A)
Paraguay*	7/1/68	2/4/70	
Peru*	7/1/68	3/3/70	
Philippines*	7/1/68	10/5/72	
Poland*	7/1/68	6/12/69	
Portugal*			12/15/77(A)
Qatar			4/3/89(A)
Romania	7/1/68	2/4/70	

---

[3] Extended to Netherlands Antilles and Aruba.

Country	Date of Signature	Date of Deposit of Ratification	Date of Deposit of Accession (A) or Succession (S)
Russia[4]	7/1/68	3/5/70	
Rwanda			5/20/75(A)
St. Kitts and Nevis			3/22/93(A)
St. Lucia*			12/28/79(S)
St. Vincent & the Grenadines			11/6/84(S)
San Marino	7/1/68	8/10/70	
Sao Tome and Principe			7/20/83(A)
Saudi Arabia			10/3/88(A)
Senegal*	7/1/68	12/17/70	
Seychelles			3/12/85(A)
Sierra Leone			2/26/75(A)
Singapore*	2/5/70	3/10/76	
Slovakia			1/1/93(S)
Slovenia			4/7/92(A)
Solomon Islands			6/17/81(S)
Somalia	7/1/68	3/5/70	
South Africa*			7/10/91(A)
Spain*			11/5/87(A)
Sri Lanka*	7/1/68	3/5/79	
Sudan*	12/24/68	10/31/73	
Suriname*			6/30/76(S)
Swaziland*	6/24/69	12/11/69	
Sweden*	8/19/68	1/9/70	
Switzerland*	11/27/69	3/9/77 [1]	
Syrian Arab Republic	7/1/68	9/24/69	
Tanzania			5/31/91(A)
Thailand*			12/2/72(A)
Togo	7/1/68	2/26/70	
Tonga			7/7/71(S)
Trinidad & Tobago	8/20/68	10/30/86	
Tunisia*	7/1/68	2/26/70	
Turkey*	1/28/69	4/17/80 [1]	
Tuvalu*			1/19/79(S)
Uganda			10/20/82(A)

---

[4]   Russia has given notice that it would continue to exercise the rights and fulfill the obligations of the former Soviet Union arising from the NPT.

Country	Date of Signature	Date of Deposit of Ratification	Date of Deposit of Accession (A) or Succession (S)
United Kingdom	7/1/68	11/27/68 [5]	
United States	7/1/68	3/5/70	
Uruguay*	7/1/68	8/31/70	
Uzbekistan			5/2/92
Venezuela*	7/1/68	9/25/75	
Vietnam,* Socialist Rep of			6/14/82 (A)
Western Samoa*			3/17/75 (A)
Yemen[6]	11/14/68	6/1/79	
Zaire*	7/22/68	8/4/70	
Zambia			5/15/91 (A)
Zimbabwe			9/26/91 (A)
Taiwan[7]	7/1/68	1/27/70	

TOTAL: 163 (Total does not include Taiwan)

---

[5] Extended to Aguilla and territories under the territorial sovereignty of the United Kingdom.

[6] The Republic of Yemen resulted from the union of the Yemen Arab Republic and the People's Democratic Republic of Yemen. The table indicates the date of signature and ratification by the People's Democratic Republic of Yemen, the first of these two states to become a party to the NPT. The Yemen Arab Republic signed the NPT on 9/23/68 and deposited its instrument of ratification on 5/14/86.

[7] On 1/27/70, an instrument of ratification was deposited in the name of the Republic of China. Effective 1/1/79, the United States recognized the People's Republic of China as the sole legal government of China. The authorities on Taiwan state that they will continue to abide by the provisions of the Treaty and United States regards them as bound by the obligations imposed by the Treaty.

Notes

Editors' Introduction

1.   Report to the UN and the UN Disarmament Commission of August 28, 1968, ENDC/236, *Documents on Disarmament, 1968*, pp. 591,593.

2.   David Koplow's paper was written in 1992, before the Clinton administration supported the resumption of CTB negotiations in the CD and made the achievement of a CTB a first-order priority. Nevertheless, Koplow's paper contains research relevant to the NPT extension conference in 1995, and to the achievement of associated arms control agreements well after 1995, and is therefore included in this volume.

3.   Statement by the Press Secretary, the White House Office of the Press Secretary, Mar. 15, 1994.

4.   R. Jeffrey Smith, "Clinton Decides to Retain Bush Nuclear Arms Policy," *The Washington Post* (Sept. 22), 1994, pp. A1, A26.

5.   See, "Preparing for the 1995 NPT Conference: ACT Interviews Thomas Graham, Jr.," *Arms Control Today* 24 (July/Aug. 1994), p. 12.

6.   R. Jeffrey Smith, *op cit.*

7.   For examples of this argument, see Secretary of Defense Les Aspin's speech to the National Academy of Sciences on December 7, 1993 announcing the new U.S. counterproliferation policy; Mark Dean Millot, "Facing the Emerging Reality of Regional Nuclear Adversaries," *The Washington Quarterly* (Summer 1994); and Peter W. Rodman, "A Grown-Ups Guide to Non-Proliferation," *The National Review* (July 5, 1993).

8.   Wolfgang K.H. Panofsky and George Bunn, "The Doctrine of the Nuclear-Weapon States and the Future of Non-Proliferation," *Arms Control Today* 24 (July/Aug. 1994), pp. 3–9. (Emphasis in the original.)

Chapter 1: Nuclear Disarmament

1.   The full text of Article VI reads:

> Each of the Parties to the Treaty undertakes to pursue negotiations in good faith on effective measures relating to cessation of the nuclear arms race at an early date and to nuclear disarmament, and on a treaty on

general and complete disarmament under strict and effective international control.

2. The 1967 date comes from the NPT: Art.IX.3 defines "nuclear-weapon state," for the purposes of the treaty, as one "which has manufactured and exploded a nuclear weapon or other nuclear explosive device prior to January 1, 1967." That included only the five mentioned in the text. The NPT's purpose was to prevent increases in this number if that was possible. The 1961 "Irish resolution," the UN General Assembly resolution that was the origin of the NPT negotiations, sought a treaty in which nuclear-weapon states would promise not to disseminate nuclear weapons or information on their manufacture, and non-nuclear-weapon states "would undertake not to manufacture or otherwise acquire control of such weapons." UNGA Res. 1665 (XVI), Dec. 4, 1961. See G. Bunn, *Arms Control by Committee: Managing Negotiations with the Russians* (Stanford University Press, 1992), pp. 64–66.

3. See NPT Arts. VI, VII.3 and X.

4. See, e.g., Soviet Proposal Submitted to the Eighteen-Nation Disarmament Committee: Draft Treaty on General and Complete Disarmament Under Strict International Control, Mar. 15, 1962, ACDA, *Documents on Disarmament, 1962*, pp. 103–127; U.S. Proposal Submitted to the Eighteen-Nation Disarmament Committee: Outline of Basic Provisions of a Treaty on General and Complete Disarmament in a Peaceful World, April 18, 1962, ACDA, *Documents on Disarmament, 1962*, pp. 351–382.

5. See U.S. proposal, cited above, pp. 352–53, 367–68, 374–75, 380–81.

6. One meaning for "disarm" is to "reduce armed forces." See *Webster's Ninth New Collegiate Dictionary* (Merriam-Webster, 1986), p. 359.

7. NPT, 8th preambular paragraph, (emphasis added).

8. NPT, 11th preambular paragraph, (emphasis added).

9. Dept. of State Telegram 13195 to NATO capitals, Feb. 28, 1962, National Security Archive (NSA), Nuclear Non-Proliferation Collection.

10. Dept. of State Telegram 01153 to NATO capitals of Mar. 2, 1962, NSA, NNP Collection.

11. See George Bunn, *Arms Control by Committee: Managing Negotiations with the Russians* (Stanford University Press, 1992), p. 66.

12. See George Bunn and Charles N. Van Doren, "Options for Extension of the NPT: the Intention of the Drafters of Article X.2," in Bunn, Fischer and Van Doren, *Options & Opportunities: The NPT Extension Conference of 1995* (Programme for Promoting Nuclear Non-Proliferation, 1991), pp. 3–6.

13. Bunn and Van Doren, cited above, p. 5.

14. Memorandum of the Federal Republic of Germany to other governments, April 7, 1967, ACDA, *Documents on Disarmament, 1967*, pp. 179, 180, 182.

15. ACDA, *International Negotiations on the Treaty on the Non-Proliferation of Nuclear Weapons* (GPO, 1969), pp. 133, 135.

16. Italian Proposal Submitted to the Eighteen Nation Disarmament

Committee: Draft of Unilateral Nonacquisition Declaration, September 14, 1965, *Documents on Disarmament, 1965* (1966), p. 411–12.

17. ACDA, *Documents on Disarmament, 1965,* p. 424–25 (emphasis added).

18. UNGA Res. 2028 of Nov. 19, 1965, ACDA, *Documents on Disarmament, 1965,* pp. 532–34.

19. Statement of March 3, 1966, ACDA, *Documents on Disarmament, 1966,* pp. 68, 77 (emphasis added).

20. Memorandum of Aug. 19, 1966, ACDA, *Documents on Disarmament, 1966,* pp. 576–78.

21. Mexican Working Paper of Sept. 19, 1967, ACDA, *Documents on Disarmament, 1967,* pp. 394–95.

22. Brazilian Amendments of October 31, 1967, *Documents on Disarmament, 1967,* p. 546; Statement of the Burmese representative of Oct. 10, 1967, *Documents, 1967,* p. 459, 463; Statement of Indian Delegate of Sept. 28, 1967, *Documents, 1967,* pp. 430, 440; Rumanian Working Paper of October 19, 1967, *Documents, 1967,* pp. 525–26; Swiss Aide-Memoire of Nov. 17, 1967, *Documents, 1967,* pp. 572–574.

23. Statement of Feb. 24, 1967 ENDC/PV.289.

24. Statement to the Diet, Mar. 14, 1967.

25. Statement of Feb. 23, 1967, ENDC/PV.288 (emphasis added).

26. Bunn and Van Doren, cited above, at pp. 5–8.

27. Revised identical American and Soviet NPT drafts of Jan. 18, 1968, in ACDA, *International Negotiation of the Treaty on the Non-Proliferation of Nuclear Weapons* (GPO, 1969), pp. 150, 153–54. The earlier Soviet and U.S. drafts also appear in this book.

28. ACDA, *International Negotiations,* cited above, at pp. 150–59. These changes appeared in drafts of Jan. 18, 1968 and March 11, 1968.

29. U.N. Charter, chap. VII.

30. NPT Art. X.1.

31. Statement of April 26, 1968, ACDA, *Documents on Disarmament, 1968,* p. 230–231 (emphasis added).

32. David A. Koplow, "Passing Good Faith: Has the United States Violated Article VI of the Nuclear Non-Proliferation Treaty?" 1993 *Wis. Law Review,* pp. 301, 367–374.

33. Statement of July 1, 1968, ACDA, *Documents on Disarmament, 1968,* pp. 458–60.

34. Memorandum of July 1, 1968, ACDA, *Documents on Disarmament, 1968,* pp. 466–70.

35. Report to the United Nations and the UN Disarmament Commission of August 28, 1968, ENDC/236, ACDA, *Documents on Disarmament, 1968,* pp. 591, 593.

36. These included Australia, Germany, Japan, Indonesia, Turkey and Yugoslavia.

37. Warren H. Donnelly & Robert L. Beckman, "Nuclear Non-Proliferation Treaty Conference," reprinted in Environment and Natural Resources Policy Division of the Congressional Research Service, 99th Cong., 1st Sess., *Nuclear Proliferation Factbook*, p. 577, 581 (1985).

38. Final Declaration of the Review Conference of the Parties to the Treaty on the Non-Proliferation of Nuclear Weapons, May 30, 1975, ACDA, *Documents on Disarmament, 1975*, pp. 146, 153–155.

39. Working paper submitted by the Group of 77 non-aligned countries on Aug. 26, 1980. NPT/CONF. II/C.I/2.

40. Final Document of the Tenth Special Session of the General Assembly, June 30, 1978, ACDA, *Documents on Disarmament, 1978*, pp. 411, 420–21 (emphasis added).

41. Final Declaration by the Third Review Conference of the Parties to the Treaty on the Non-Proliferation of Nuclear Weapons, Sept. 21, 1985. ACDA, *Documents on Disarmament, 1985*, pp. 641, 650–56.

42. Mohamed I. Shaker, "The Legacy of the 1985 Nuclear Non-Proliferation Treaty Review Conference: The President's Reflections [Shaker was president of the conference]," in John Simpson, ed., *Nuclear Non-Proliferation: An Agenda for the 1990s* (Cambridge, UK: Cambridge University Press, 1987), pp. 9,10,15 (emphasis added).

43. Charles N. Van Doren and George Bunn, "Progress and Peril at the Fourth NPT Review Conference," *Arms Control Today* (Oct. 1990), p. 89.

44. See George Bunn and Roland Timerbaev, "Security Assurances to Non-Nuclear-Weapon States," *The Nonproliferation Review*, v.1, no.1 (Fall 1993), p. 11.

45. UNGA Res.48/75L (1993); Statement of President Clinton to UNGA, Sept. 27, 1993; White House Fact Sheet on nuclear issues dated Sept. 27, 1993; Joint Statement by the President of the Russian Federation and the President of the United States on the Non-Proliferation of Weapons of Mass Destruction and the Means of their Delivery dated January 14, 1994.

46. For a report showing the current differences of views at the Geneva conference on this subject, see "Report of the Ad Hoc Committee on Effective International Arrangements to Assure Non-Nuclear-Weapon States against the Use or Threat of Use of Nuclear Weapons," Conference on Disarmament, CD/1219, August 25, 1993.

47. See Bunn and Timerbaev, "Security Assurances . . . ," cited above.

48. For an argument that, until the United States agreed to resume negotiations for a comprehensive test ban, it was in violation of Article VI, see Koplow, "Passing Good Faith . . . ," cited above.

49. Doc. CD/1231.

50. See G. Bunn, "The Non-Proliferation Treaty of 1968 and its Extension in 1995," *Nonproliferation Review* (published by the Monterey Institute for International Studies) Winter 1994, v.1, no.2, pp, 51–60.

51. See Bunn and Van Doren, "Options for Extension . . . ," cited above, p. 10.

52. Cf. William Epstein, "Amendment Conference is Best Way to Achieve Early CTBT & Help NPT," *Disarmament Times* (Dec. 21, 1993), p. 4.

53. See Lewis Dunn, "NPT 1995: Time to Shift Gears," *Arms Control Today* 23 (November 1994), pp. 14–19.

54. For an argument that such a recess would not bring the NPT to an end, see Bunn and Van Doren, "Options for Extension . . . ," cited above, pp. 9–10. For further discussion, see Serge Sur, "The problem of the continuance in force of the NPT after 1995 in the absence of a decision extending the Treaty—UNIDIR/91/52" and the reply from David Fischer, "Postscript-Some Comments on Professor Sur's Note," both in Bunn, Fischer and Van Doren, "Options & Opportunities . . . ," cited above.

55. The total Russian and U.S. land-based and sea-based strategic nuclear missile warheads (not counting gravity bombs or cruise missiles launched from aircraft) will be about 2,200 each if START II is fully implemented. *New York Times*, Dec. 30, 1992, table entitled "Limiting Nuclear Warheads." These were what seemed the most threatening warheads during the mid-1960s when the NPT was negotiated, and are therefore the most important from the viewpoint of Art. VI. At the end of 1969, at the beginning of the SALT negotiations just before the NPT went into effect, the number of Soviet and U.S. strategic missile warheads that both sides assumed would be frozen if SALT produced an immediate freeze was under 2,000, including all those deployed and in the "pipeline." Lawrence D. Weiler, *The Arms Race, Secret Negotiations and Congress* (Occasional Paper No. 12, Stanley Foundation, 1976), p. 16.

56. For non-governmental proposals for drastic reductions in, and elimination of, national nuclear arsenals, see Gerard C. Smith, "Take Nuclear Weapons into Custody," *Bulletin of the Atomic Scientists*, December 1990; Roger D. Speed, "International Control of Nuclear Weapons" (Center for International Security and Arms Control, Stanford University, publication forthcoming in 1994); Joseph Rotblat, Jack Steinberger and Bhalchandra Udgaonkar, eds., *A Nuclear-Weapon-Free World* (Westview Press, 1993); Edward Teller, "Revival of the Baruch Plan," January 1992 (unpublished memorandum); Robert S. McNamara, "The Changing Nature of Global Security and its Impact on South Asia," Address to the Indian Defence Policy Forum, November 20, 1992, A publication of the Washington Council on Non-Proliferation; Andrew J. Goodpaster, *"Further Reins on Nuclear Arms: Next Steps for the Major Nuclear Powers"*, The Atlantic Council, Consultation Paper Series, August 1993; Roland Timerbaev, "Nonproliferation Organizations and Regimes Beyond 1995," (to be published in 1994 in *Beyond 1995?* by the Center for National Security Studies, Los Alamos National Laboratory).

Chapter 2: Two Options for the NPT Extension Conference

1. This was part of a monograph entitled *Options and Opportunities: The NPT Extension Conference of 1995* (Programme for Promoting Nuclear Non-Proliferation, 1991) to which we and David Fischer contributed.

2. See Annex 1 by David Fischer to the article cited above, "Article X.2 of the Nuclear Non-Proliferation Treaty and the Nature of its 1995 Extension

Conference" in Bunn, Van Doren and Fischer, *Options and Opportunities . . .* , pp. 36–38 and, for Fischer's reply, p. 35.

3. *Ibid,* pp. 2–10. The judicial opinion is Commission v. France, (1971), E.C.R. 1003 holding that provisional extension had taken place beyond the seven-year period set in a treaty that said: "Seven years after entry into force of this Treaty, the Council may confirm these provisions in their entirety. Failing confirmation, new provisions relating to the subject matter of this Chapter shall be adopted . . . ." The multilateral EC Council had been unable to reach agreement on confirming the old provisions or adopting any new ones during the seven years or during more than six years afterwards. The Court nevertheless held the treaty to have been provisionally extended and to be still in force.

4. *Ibid,* pp. 35–38.

5. *Ibid,* p. 35.

6. Vienna Convention on the Law of Treaties of 1969, Articles 54 and 57. Article 56 provides that a treaty "which contains no provision regarding termination and which does not provide for denunciation or withdrawal is not subject to denunciation or withdrawal unless: (a) it is established that the parties intended to admit the possibility of denunciation or withdrawal; or (b) a right of denunciation or withdrawal may be implied by the nature of the treaty." The Vienna Convention has not been ratified by the United States but is regarded as reflecting customary international law and practice by the United States and many other countries.

7. Sometimes conclusion of a succeeding treaty implies termination of the predecessor, and sometimes a party can suspend its obligations because of material breach by another party, supervening impossibility of performance or fundamental change of circumstances. See Vienna Convention, Articles 59–62.

8. Article 32.

9. See Bunn and Van Doren, "Options for Extension . . . ," pp. 2–3.

10. *Ibid,* pp. 3–9.

11. Geneva's telegram 881 to the U.S. State Dept., Aug. 25, 1966, National Security Archives, Nuclear Non-Proliferation Collection (Washington, D.C, 1992).

12. See Bunn and Van Doren, "Options for Extension . . . ," pp. 3–6.

13. Statement of Italian Representative Caracciolo to the Eighteen-Nation Disarmament Committee, the multilateral Geneva disarmament conference, of Nov. 23, 1967, ENDC/PV.350, p. 6. A similar amendment with "twenty-five" replacing "X" was submitted by Italy on Feb. 20, 1968, just after the U.S.-Soviet draft containing the revised Art.X.2 discussed above was submitted to the Geneva conference. Italian Working Paper, ENDC/218 and Corr.2, U.S. Arms Control and Disarmament Agency (ACDA), *Documents on Disarmament, 1968,* p. 92. Earlier versions of the Italian idea appear in Bunn and Van Doren, "Options for Extension . . . ," pp. 3–6.

14. U.S. Mission Geneva's telegram 1300 to Washington, Oct. 21, 1967, declassified as a result of Freedom of Information Act request, ACDA Case No. 91029, Nov. 12, 1991.

15. Geneva's 1300 to the Dept. of State.

16. *Ibid.*

17. U.S. Mission Geneva's telegram 6088 to U.S. Dept. of State, Nov. 17, 1967, also declassified in ACDA's Case No. 91029.

18. The U.S. Mission to NATO agreed with Fisher on the language he recommended, since it would be most acceptable to U.S. allies, adding: "Italy and FRG have made it known to U.S. on number of occasions that `satisfactory' NPT duration clause, i.e., one limited to 25 or 20 years, and probably more like 10 years, is of major concern to them." U.S. Mission to NATO's telegram 529 to Dept of State, Nov. 21, 1967, declassified in ACDA Case No. 91029.

19. Geneva's 1300 to Dept. of State. (Emphasis added.)

20. See American Law Institute, *Restatement of the Law, Second, Foreign Relations Law of the United States* (ALI, 1965). See, e.g., sections 138 and 139; section 153, comments a; and b; section 155, comment c; section 156, comment c; section 158.

21. See the *Restatement...* citations in the preceding note.

22. ACDA, *Documents on Disarmament, 1968*, pp. 78, 87.

23. Authority to propose Fisher's recommended draft appears in State Dept's telegram O76978 of Nov. 29, 1967 to U.S. Mission Geneva (drafted by G. Bunn). The Soviet response appears in U.S. Mission Geneva's telegram 2274 to State Dept. of Jan. 16, 1968. Both were declassified in ACDA Case No. 91029.

24. Geneva's 1300 to the Dept. of State.

25. U.S. Mission Geneva's telegram 2281 to U.S. State Dept., Jan. 16, 1968.

26. Statement of January 18, 1968, ENDC/PV.357, 14-21 and Cor.1; ACDA, *Documents on Disarmament, 1968*, pp. 11, 16.

27. See Bunn and Van Doren, *Options and Opportunities . . .*, pp. 3–8, 10–12.

28. Statement of March 11, 1968, ENDC/PV.376, pp. 11-14; ACDA *Documents on Disarmament, 1968*, pp. 172-73.

29. Statement of March 13, 1968, ENDC/PV.378, pp. 4-10, ACDA, *Documents on Disarmament, 1969*, pp. 186, 189.

Chapter 3: Strengthening Non-Proliferation Security Assurances

1. For related approaches, see Jonathan Dean, "Expanding the Security Council Role in Blocking the Spread of Nuclear Weapons," *Transnational Law and Contemporary Problems* 2 (University of Iowa College of Law, 1992); Lewis A. Dunn, "Fifty Years Since Stagg Field: Nuclear Non-Proliferation Challenges and Opportunities," (November 1992); Lewis A.

Dunn, *Containing Nuclear Proliferation*, Adelphi Paper 263 (IISS, Winter 1991), pp. 43–44, 54–55.

The recently completed Chemical Weapons Convention uses a different approach, probably in part because of the difference between chemical and nuclear weapons, and in part because, unlike the NPT, the Convention does not distinguish between weapon "have" nations (with the five avowed nuclear-weapon countries all permanent members of the Security Council) and weapon "have not" nations. The Convention would prohibit the use, as well as the production, of chemical weapons. It contains provisions dealing with assistance for parties threatened by chemical weapons, including detection, protective and decontaminating equipment, antidotes, etc. (Article X). In case of violations threatening serious damage to the object of the Convention (e.g., use of chemical weapons on a party), a conference of the parties may recommend "collective measures" and bring the issue to the attention of the UN General Assembly and Security Council. (Article XII, 3–4.) However, no explicit suggestion for Security Council use of force to deter or counter a threat or use of chemical weapons against a party appears in the Convention. For the text and several illuminating articles about the Convention, see *Arms Control Today* 21 (October 1992).

2.   George Bunn and Charles N. Van Doren, "Two Options for the 1995 NPT Extension Conference Revisited." (Lawyers Alliance for World Security, 1992), p. 7. George Bunn and Charles N. Van Doren, "Options for Extension of the NPT: The Intention of the Drafters of Article X.2," in George Bunn, David A. Fischer and Charles N. Van Doren, *Options and Opportunities: The NPT Extension Conference of 1995* (Programme for Promoting Nuclear Non-Proliferation 1991), pp. 3–6.

3.   The NPT negotiations are described in Mohamed Shaker, *The Nuclear Non-Proliferation Treaty: Origin and Implementation, 1959–1979* (Oceana, 1980), chap. 8; and in George Bunn, *Arms Control by Committee: Managing Negotiations with the Russians* (Stanford University Press, 1992), chaps. 4-5.

4.   Shortly after the Chinese test in 1964, President Johnson announced that countries that did not seek nuclear weapons could be sure that "if they need our strong support against some threat of nuclear blackmail, then they will have it." U.S. ACDA, *Documents on Disarmament*, p. 468. During 1965, non-aligned countries began asking that the NPT include positive and negative security assurances. U.S. ACDA, *International Negotiation on the Treaty on the Non-Proliferation of Nuclear Weapons* (GPO, 1969), p. 21. In 1966, Soviet Premier Alexei Kosygin proposed that the NPT include a "clause on the prohibition of the use of nuclear weapons against non-nuclear States parties to the treaty, which have no nuclear weapons in their territory." DCOR Supp. for 1966, Doc. DC/228, Ann. 1, Sec. F (ENDC/167, February 3, 1966); Mohamed Shaker, *The Nuclear NPT . . .*, pp. 474–75. This would have left the Soviets free to threaten nuclear weapons against the Federal Republic of Germany, even if it joined the NPT, unless U.S. nuclear weapons were removed from its territory. This proposal was opposed by the United States. Later, the U.S. delegation privately asked the Soviets whether they could agree on language for a declaration or resolution to accompany the NPT based upon the formula of the 1967 Latin American nuclear-free-zone treaty (Treaty of Tlatelolco) which promises not to use or threaten to use nuclear weapons against parties observing a treaty commitment not to

acquire nuclear weapons. In early 1968, the Soviets replied that they could not accept that formula because of the existence of American nuclear weapons in Germany. Memorandum of conversation, George Bunn with Yuli Vorontsov, 15 February 1968, declassified under Freedom of Information Act.

5.   See UN Security Council Resolution 255 of June 19, 1968; "U.S. Declaration on Security Assurances to Non-Nuclear Nations" of June 17, 1968, UN Security Council verbatim, S/PV.1430, pp. 22–26. For the substantially identical Soviet and U.K. statements, see *ibid*, pp. 11–15, 17–20. A brief history of the resolution and declarations appears in U.S. Arms Control Disarmament Agency, *Arms Control and Disarmament Agreements*, (ACDA, 1990), pp. 93–94.

6.   See, e.g., Nigeria's draft treaty dealing with negative assurances. Conference on Disarmament Document CD/967, February 14, 1990.

7.   The history of the long effort by non-nuclear-weapon countries to strengthen the assurances given in 1968, in particular to add promises not to use nuclear weapons against countries that do not have them, is given in Thomas Bernauer, *Nuclear Issues on the Agenda of the Conference on Disarmament*, (United Nations Institute for Disarmament Research, 1991), chap. 1. [Hereafter cited as *Nuclear Issues . . . .*]

8.   See, e.g., "Report of the Nuclear Assurances Working Group in the Report of the Conference on Disarmament to the General Assembly of the United Nations for 1990," (CD/1039, August 30, 1990). The United States and all the other permanent members of the Security Council have acceded to a protocol to the Latin American nuclear-free zone treaty, the Treaty of Tlatelolco, in which they "undertake not to use or threaten to use nuclear weapons against Contracting Parties" to that treaty. Additional Protocol II to the Treaty for the Prohibition of Nuclear Weapons in Latin America was signed by the U.S. on April 1, 1968. The U.S. explained its adherence to this obligation with an understanding saying it would "have to consider that an armed attack by a Contracting Party, in which it was assisted by a nuclear-weapons state, would be incompatible with the Contracting Party's corresponding obligations under Article I of the Treaty [not acquire nuclear weapons `by any means whatsoever' and not to deploy them 'directly or indirectly by the Parties themselves or by anyone on their behalf.']" See U.S. Arms Control and Disarmament Agency, *Arms Control and Disarmament Agreements*, (ACDA, 1990), pp. 64–83.

9.   For the texts, see Bernauer, *Nuclear Issues . . . ,* pp. 6–10. The Russian and U.S. statements are quoted later in this paper. The Chinese non-use statement is the broadest. After stating that it would not use nuclear weapons first under any circumstances, China announced that it "undertakes unconditionally not to use nuclear weapons against non-nuclear countries and nuclear-free zones." The British and French statements have qualifications relating to NATO that are similar to the American statement quoted below.

10.   See footnote no. 8.

11.   See footnote no. 4.

12.   The text appears in U.S. ACDA *Arms Control and Disarmament Agreements*, (ACDA, 1990) p. 94 and Bernauer, *Nuclear Issues . . . ,* p. 9.

13. Bernauer, *Nuclear Issues* . . . , p. 8.

14. "Declaration on a Transformed North Atlantic Alliance" issued by the Heads of State and Government participating in the meeting of the North Atlantic Council in London, July 5 and 6, 1990, para. 20, Conference on Disarmament (CD) Doc. 1013; "The Alliance's New Strategic Concept" agreed by the Heads of State and Government participating in the meeting of the North Atlantic Council in Rome, November 7 and 8, 1991, 6 *NATO Review* (December 1991), pp. 25–32. At this meeting, the alliance reaffirmed its decision to reduce its nuclear forces by eighty per cent. See, U.S. Department of State, *Dispatch* (November 1991), p. 826. NATO's Nuclear Planning Group agreed that "there was no longer any requirement for nuclear ground-launched short-range ballistic missiles and artillery." See, Communique for meeting in Taormina, Italy, October 17 and 18, 1991, 6 *NATO Review* (December 1991), p. 33. Presidents Bush and Gorbachev agreed to withdraw to their own territories all nuclear weapons of these kinds and to dismantle the warheads. "A New Era of Reciprocal Arms Reductions," Texts of Bush and Gorbachev statements of September 27, 1991 and October 5, 1991, *Arms Control Today* 21 (October 1991), p. 3–6. U.S. and Soviet intermediate-range nuclear missiles capable of reaching Russia from U.S. allies' territory in Western Europe or reaching these allies from Warsaw Pact countries' territory had already been destroyed pursuant to the Intermediate Nuclear Forces (INF) Treaty. See also "Comparison of U.S. and Russian Nuclear Cuts," Fact Sheet of the Arms Control Association, March 6, 1992.

15. National Academy of Sciences, *The Future of the U.S.-Soviet Nuclear Relationship* (National Academy Press, 1991), pp. 23–24.

16. See, e.g., Thomas C. Reed, "The Role of Nuclear Weapons in the New World Order," briefing by the Chairman of the JSTPS/SAG Deterrence Study Group, October 10, 1991.

17. See, e.g., Michael M. May and Roger D. Speed, "Should Nuclear Weapons Be Used?" (Unpublished manuscript, September 1, 1992).

18. Remarks by Secretary of State James Baker, April 28, 1992.

19. See "Lisbon Protocol to the Strategic Arms Reduction Treaty (START)", *Arms Control Today.* Washington, DC: Arms Control Association, June 1992.

20. "Remarks by the President in Address to the United Nations General Assembly," New York City, September 21, 1992, White House press release.

21. See footnote no. 9.

Chapter 4: Nuclear Testing and the Non-Proliferation Treaty

1. Treaty on the Non-Proliferation of Nuclear Weapons, July 1, 1968, 21 U.S.T. 483, T.I.A.S. No. 6839, 729 U.N.T.S. 161 [hereinafter NPT].

2. Regarding the dangers of the proliferation of modern weapons, and the legal responses to help constrain those perils, see: David Dewitt, ed., *Nuclear Non-Proliferation and Global Security* (St. Martin's Press, 1987);

David Fischer, *Stopping the Spread of Nuclear Weapons: The Past and the Prospects* (Routledge, 1992); William Epstein, *The Last Chance: Nuclear Proliferation and Arms Control* (Free Press, 1976); and J. Pilat and R. Pendley, eds., *Beyond 1995: The Future of the NPT Regime* (Plenum Press, 1990).

3. The International Atomic Energy Agency is a multilateral body, headquartered in Vienna, which operates the international system of "safeguards"—bookkeeping procedures, physical tags and seals, on-site inspection, etc.—to monitor compliance with non-proliferation standards. See Lawrence Scheinman, *The International Atomic Energy Agency and World Nuclear Order* (Resources for the Future, 1987); David Fischer and Paul Szasz, *Safeguarding the Atom: A Critical Appraisal* (Taylor and Francis, 1985).

4. Article IX.3 of the NPT defines a "nuclear weapon state" as a country "which has manufactured and exploded a nuclear weapon or other nuclear device prior to January 1, 1967." Under this definition, the United States, the Soviet Union (and Russia as its successor state for this purpose), the United Kingdom, France, and China count as NWS. India has conducted one nuclear explosion, in 1974.

5. Charles N. Van Doren and George Bunn, "Progress and Peril at the Fourth NPT Review Conference," *Arms Control Today* 21 (Oct. 1990), p. 8; Leonard Spector and Jacqueline Smith, "Deadlock Damages Nonproliferation," *Bulletin of the Atomic Scientists* (Dec. 1990), p. 39.

6. Article X.2 provides that "Twenty-five years after the entry into force of the Treaty, a conference shall be convened to decide whether the Treaty shall continue in force indefinitely, or shall be extended for an additional fixed period or periods. This decision shall be taken by a majority of the Parties to the Treaty."

7. Thomas Graham, Jr., "The Duration of the Nuclear Non-Proliferation Treaty: Sudden Death or New Lease on Life?," 1989 *Virginia Journal of International Law*; George Bunn and Charles N. Van Doren, "Options for Extension of the NPT: the Intention of the Drafters of Article X.2," in Bunn, Fisher, and Van Doren, *Options & Opportunities: The NPT Extension Conference of 1995* (Programme for Promoting Nuclear Non-Proliferation, 1991); Bunn and Van Doren, "Two Options for the 1995 NPT Extension Conference Revisited," (Lawyers Alliance for World Security, Issue Brief, July 1992).

8. A persistent NNWS could probably manage to construct a crude atomic bomb, and have confidence in its reliability, without conducting even a single nuclear test explosion. The United States never tested the type of atomic bomb dropped on Hiroshima at the end of World War II, and Israel has perhaps never tested any of its weapons. The more general practice, however, has been to test nuclear devices thoroughly before deploying them and a sustained test program would surely be necessary to proceed with development of a sophisticated arsenal of hydrogen bombs.

9. Treaty Banning Nuclear Weapon Tests in the Atmosphere, in Outer Space and Under Water, Aug. 5, 1963, 14 U.S.T. 1313, T.I.A.S. No. 5433, 480 U.N.T.S. 43 [hereinafter LTBT].

10. Regarding the history of the LTBT, see Glenn Seaborg and Benjamin Loeb, *Kennedy, Khrushchev and the Test Ban* (University of California Press, 1981).

11. In addition, in Article I of the LTBT, immediately after the passage proscribing nuclear testing in three environments while permitting them to continue underground, the parties stated, "[i]t is understood in this connection that the provisions of this subparagraph are without prejudice to the conclusion of a treaty resulting in the permanent banning of all nuclear test explosions, including all such explosions underground, the conclusion of which, as the Parties have stated in the Preamble to this Treaty, they seek to achieve."

12. Treaty on the Limitation of Underground Nuclear Weapon Tests, July 3, 1974, United States-U.S.S.R., 13 I.L.M. 907 [hereinafter TTBT].

13. Treaty on Underground Nuclear Explosions for Peaceful Purposes, May 28, 1976, United States-U.S.S.R., 15 I.L.M. 893 [hereinafter PNET].

14. The size of a nuclear weapon is traditionally measured in "kilotons" of yield, assessing its destructive power against the detonation of a comparable number of thousands of tons of TNT high explosive. A one hundred fifty kiloton weapon is approximately ten times as powerful as the bomb dropped on Hiroshima.

15. Herbert York, *Making Weapons, Talking Peace: A Physicist's Odyssey from Hiroshima to Geneva* (Basic Books, 1987), pp. 282-323.

16. Lloyd Jensen, *Negotiating Nuclear Arms Control* (University of South Carolina Press, 1988), p. 43.

17. The process for bringing the TTBT and PNET into force was exceptionally extended. The TTBT was signed in 1974, but by its terms was to await the conclusion of the PNET, which occurred in 1976. President Ford then submitted both treaties to the Senate, but President Carter opted to defer the ratification process, since he was hoping to conclude a prompt CTBT that would supersede them. When the Reagan administration took office, the CTBT talks were terminated; the United States later insisted that the verification provisions for the two pending treaties must be augmented prior to their entry into force. The negotiations over those enhancements produced two lengthy protocols in 1990; the Senate then provided its advice and consent, and all four documents entered into force in December, 1990.

18. Letter from President Reagan to the Chairs of the Senate and House Armed Services Committees, Oct. 10, 1986, ACDA, *Documents on Disarmament, 1986*, pp. 624, 625.

19. R. Jeffrey Smith, "Breaking Pledge, U.S. to Defer Underground Nuclear Test Talks," *The Washington Post* (Jan. 24, 1990), p. 24.

20. R. Jeffrey Smith, "Negotiators Face Hurdles on Range of Arms Issues," *The Washington Post* (Sept. 20, 1987), p. A20.

21. Hearing on National Security Implications of Nuclear Testing Agreements before the Senate Committee on Armed Services, 101st Congress, 2d session, (Sept. 17, 1990), pp. 20–21.

22. Philip Schrag, *Global Action: Nuclear Test Ban Diplomacy at the End of the Cold War* (Westview Press, 1992).

23. "Known Nuclear Tests Worldwide, 1945 to December 31, 1991," *Bulletin of the Atomic Scientists* (Apr. 1992), p. 49.

24. For histories of the negotiation and implementation of the NPT, see Mohamed I. Shaker, *The Nuclear Non-Proliferation Treaty: Origin and Implementation 1959-1979* (Oceana, 1980); Glenn Seaborg, *Stemming the Tide: Arms Control in the Johnson Years* (Lexington Press, 1987); and Mason Willrich, *Non-Proliferation Treaty: Framework for Nuclear Arms Control* (Michie Press Co., 1969).

25. Vienna Convention on the Law of Treaties, May 23, 1969, U.N. Doc. A/CONF 39/27 (in force, the U.S. is not a party) [hereinafter Vienna Convention]. The United States has not ratified the Vienna Convention, but has acknowledged that many parts of it are binding, nonetheless, as an authoritative statement of customary international law. See American Law Institute, Restatement of the Foreign Relations Law of the United States, 3d ed. (1986), Vol. 1 [hereinafter Restatement], Introductory Note to Part III, pp. 144–45.

26. Vienna Convention, footnote no. 25, arts. 31, 32. In contrast to leading international authorities (which tend to be extremely "textual", focusing attention upon the words of the document and its immediate context), leading American authorities are quicker to resort to the negotiating history as a guide to the parties' intentions in interpreting and implementing a treaty. Restatement, footnote no. 25, §325, reporters' notes 1 and 4.

27. Mexican Working Paper on the link between the provisions of the NPT regarding nuclear disarmament measures and those regarding the review conferences and the limited duration of the Treaty, Sept. 4, 1990, NPT/CONF.IV/MC.I/CRP.3 [hereinafter Mexican Paper], pp. 6–8; United States Arms Control and Disarmament Agency, *International Negotiations on the Treaty on the Nonproliferation of Nuclear Weapons* (GPO, 1969), pp. 86-88, [hereinafter ACDA History].

28. Mexican Paper, footnote no. 27, at 11–22; ACDA History, footnote no. 27, at 15, 20; William Epstein, "The Linkage Between a Nuclear Test Ban and Nuclear Non-Proliferation," in M. P. Fry, Patrick Keatinge, and Joseph Rotblat (eds.), *Nuclear Non-Proliferation and the Non-Proliferation Treaty* (1990), pp. 132, 135. ("As regards the interpretation of Article VI, it was well understood by all parties that "measures relating to cessation of the nuclear arms race" was clearly intended to cover such measures as a CTB, a ban on the production of fissionable material for weapons, a freeze on the production of additional nuclear weapons, and a ban on flight testing of delivery vehicles. While there was room for differences regarding the entire list, a CTB was at the top of everyone's list of measures, and there can be no doubt that a CTB was considered as the essential and indispensable measure for cessation of the nuclear arms race.")

29. President Johnson, for example, declared in 1966 that the United States "persists in its belief that the perils of proliferation would be materially reduced by an extension of the limited test ban Treaty to cover underground nuclear tests." Quoted in Marin-Bosch, Amendment Conference to the Partial Test-Ban Treaty, 14 Disarmament No. 2 (1991), pp. 83, 85. See also Mason Willrich, footnote 24, p. 162 (Rusk highlighting CTB as a prompt post-NPT step); ACDA History, footnote no. 27, p. 22 (statement of Ambassador Goldberg, affirming United States interest in CTB).

30. During this period, the United States and the Soviet Union were also laying the groundwork for what eventually became the SALT negotiations and they attached great importance to the opportunities to "freeze"

the nuclear arms race. Some officials inside the Johnson administration therefore accorded SALT an even higher priority than CTBT, but the maneuvering toward the opening of SALT was kept entirely behind the scenes. The American and Soviet public presentations never veered from the earnest avowal that concluding a test ban accord was a top superpower priority. See Glenn Seaborg, footnote no. 24; United States Arms Control and Disarmament Agency, "Texts and Histories of the Negotiations," *Arms Control and Disarmament Agreements* (ACDA, 1990), pp. 150–51.

31. The Final Declaration of the 1975 Review Conference contained strong language about the obligation to conclude a CTBT:

> The Conference expresses the view that the conclusion of a treaty banning all nuclear weapons tests is one of the most important measures to halt the nuclear arms race. It expresses the hope that the nuclear-weapon States Party to the Treaty will take the lead in reaching an early solution of the technical and political difficulties on this issue. It appeals to these States to make every effort to reach agreement on the conclusion of an effective comprehensive test ban.

The President of that conference, Ambassador Thorsson of Sweden, summarized the proceedings by noting:

> It seems to me that an enlightened world opinion, reflected in this case, in statements by non-nuclear-weapons states, rather impatiently awaits concrete and binding results of on-going bilateral negotiations, aiming at ending the quantitative and qualitative arms race, and reducing substantially the levels of nuclear armaments. Many have referred to the need for a time-table for results to be achieved through these negotiations. The agreement on a comprehensive test ban is clearly recognized as a most decisive element in these efforts. A least common denominator is apparent in the statements: Article VI must be implemented, in letter and in spirit.

Quoted in Warren Donnelly and Robert Beckman, Issue Brief, Congressional Research Service, April 2, 1985, reprinted in *Nuclear Proliferation Factbook*, prepared by the Environmental and Natural Resources Policy Division of the Congressional Research Service, Library of Congress, Joint Committee Print, 99th Congress, 1st session, (Aug. 1985), pp. 577, 581.

32. The Carter administration had undertaken trilateral CTBT negotiations in 1977, and they had proceeded quite far toward an accord. However, following the Soviet Union's invasion of Afghanistan in Dec. 1979, those negotiations, like all other arms control initiatives, stultified. Herbert York, footnote no. 15.

33. William Epstein, "A Critical Time for Nuclear Nonproliferation," 253 *Scientific American* No. 2 (Aug. 1985), p. 33; 5 *United Nations Disarmament Yearbook* (1981), pp. 126–47. During the 1980 Review Conference, Sigvard Eklund, Director-General of the IAEA concluded, "The non-proliferation regime can only survive on the tripod of the NPT, effective international safeguards, and a CTB. The vital third leg is still missing as it was five years ago." quoted in William Epstein, "The Nuclear Testing Threat," *Bulletin of the Atomic Scientists* (July/Aug., 1990), pp. 35, 36.

34. The Third Review Conference, in 1985, produced a remarkable final document, in which both the NNWS majority and the United States-United Kingdom minority stated their views:

> The Conference except for certain States whose views are reflected in the

following subparagraph deeply regretted that a comprehensive multilateral Nuclear Test Ban Treaty banning all nuclear tests by all States in all environments for all time had not been concluded so far and, therefore, called on the nuclear weapon States Party to the Treaty to resume trilateral negotiations in 1985 and called on all the nuclear-weapon States to participate in the urgent negotiation and conclusion of such a Treaty as a matter of the highest priority in the Conference on Disarmament.

At the same time, the Conference noted that certain States Party to the Treaty, while committed to the goal of an effectively verifiable comprehensive Nuclear Test Ban Treaty, considered deep and verifiable reductions in existing arsenals of nuclear weapons as the highest priority in the process of pursuing the objectives of Article VI.

35. The United States and Soviet Union were the co-chairs of the negotiating body (the Eighteen Nation Disarmament Committee, which subsequently evolved into today's 40-member Conference on Disarmament) and at the first session following the signing of the NPT, they proposed an agenda for the body's future work. The first item, paralleling Article VI of the new treaty, was "Further effective measures relating to the cessation of the nuclear arms race at an early date and to nuclear disarmament." The co-chairs noted that a number of initiatives might be considered under this heading and they listed CTBT first among them. (The SALT negotiations on strategic nuclear arms, being strictly bilateral between the United States and the Soviet Union, were not included on the list of multilateral agenda items.) ACDA, *Documents on Disarmament, 1968*, p. 583.

36. The Reagan and Bush administrations have continued to acknowledge that a CTBT remains a "long term objective" of the United States, but they also affirmed that "[a]s long as the United States and our friends and allies must rely upon nuclear weapons to deter aggression, however, some level of nuclear testing will continue to be necessary." United States Department of State, "U.S. Policy Regarding Limitations on Nuclear Testing," (Aug. 1986), Special Report No. 150, reprinted in ACDA, *Documents on Disarmament, 1986*, pp. 448, 451. See also Threshold Test Ban and Peaceful Nuclear Explosions Treaties with the U.S.S.R., Hearings before the Senate Foreign Relations Committee, 101st Congress, 2d session, S. Hrg. 101-1090 (1990), p. 110 (written responses from Amb. Lehman to Senator Pell).

37. A recent administration policy paper reported that:

A comprehensive test ban remains a long-term US objective. Such a ban must be viewed in the context of a time when the United States no longer needs to depend on nuclear deterrence to ensure international security and stability, and when it has achieved 1) broad, deep, and verifiable arms reductions; 2) greatly improved verification capabilities; 3) expanded confidence-building measures; and 4)greater balance in conventional forces.

Gist: US Nuclear Testing Policy, 2 US Department of State Dispatch No. 33 (August 19, 1991), pp. 626, 627.

38. R. Jeffrey Smith, "Bush Rejects Proposed Limits on Underground Nuclear Tests," *The Washington Post* (July 15, 1992), p. A16; Michael R. Gordon, "U.S. Tightens Limit on Nuclear Tests," *The New York Times* (July 15, 1992), p. A5.

39. Horgan, "Counting Down," 267 *Scientific American* No. 2 (August 1992), pp. 20–21 (citing the calculations of bomb engineer Ray E. Kidder).

40. Helen Dewar, "Senate Votes Overwhelmingly for Far-Reaching Nuclear Testing Moratorium," *The Washington Post* (Aug. 4, 1992), p. A4; R. Jeffrey Smith, "Bush Rejects Proposed Limits on Underground Nuclear Tests," *The Washington Post* (July 15, 1992), p. A16.

41. Black's Law Dictionary (5th ed. 1979) p. 623 notes that "Good faith is an intangible and abstract quality with no technical meaning or statutory definition, and it encompasses, among other things, an honest belief, the absence of malice and the absence of design to defraud or to seek an unconscionable advantage . . . ." The pervasiveness of the notion of good faith in various aspects of American law is illustrated by indexes to legal source materials, which contain citations under the heading "good faith" to dozens of areas of law, from bankruptcy to discovery to search and seizure to uniform commercial code. See Index to Annotations, ALR 2,3,4, Fed (1986); General Index, *American Jurisprudence* (2d ed. 1991).

42. 29 U.S.C. §158(a)(5); 158(b)(3) (1973 and 1992 Supp.) §158(d) defines the mutual obligation:

> to meet at reasonable times and confer in good faith with respect to wages, hours, and other terms and conditions of employment, or the negotiation of an agreement, or any question arising thereunder, and the execution of a written contract incorporating any agreement reached if requested by either party, but such obligation does not compel either party to agree to a proposal or require the making of a concession.

43. NLRB v. Reed & Price Manufacturing Co., 205 F.2d 131, 34 (1st Cir.), cert. denied, 346 U.S. 887 (1953). See also NLRB v. Insurance Agents' International Union, 361 U.S. 477, 485 (1960) (quoting early NLRB report, "the essential thing is rather the serious intent to adjust differences and to reach an acceptable common ground"); NLRB v. MacMillan Ring-Free Oil Co., 394 F.2d 26, 29 (9th Cir.), cert. denied, 393 U.S. 914 (1968).

44. NLRB v. Overnite Transportation Co., 938 F.2d 815 (7th Cir. 1991); Seattle-First National Bank v. NLRB, 638 F.2d 1221, 1226, 27 (9th Cir. 1981); NLRB v. Cable Vision, 660 F.2d 1, 3 (1st Cir. 1981); Clear Pine Moldings, Inc. v. NLRB, 632 F.2d 721 (9th Cir. 1980).

45. Vienna Convention, footnote no. 25, Article 26 (every treaty must be performed in good faith) and Article 31 (a treaty shall be interpreted in good faith).

46. See J. O'Connor, *Good Faith in International Law* (1991); Admission of a State to the United Nations, I.C.J. Reports 1948, p. 57; Case Concerning the Temple of Preah Vihear (Cambodia v. Thailand), I.C.J. Reports 1962, p. 6; South-West Africa Voting Procedure, I.C.J. Reports 1955, p. 67.

47. Railway Traffic Between Lithuania and Poland, P.C.I.J. Series A/B, No. 42 (1931), p. 108, 116; North Sea Continental Shelf Cases (Federal Republic of Germany v. Denmark and Netherlands), I.C.J. Reports 1969, p. 46:

> [T]he parties are under an obligation to enter into negotiations with a view to arriving at an agreement, and not merely to go through a formal process of negotiation as a sort of prior condition for the automatic application of a certain method of delimitation in the absence of an agreement; they are under an obligation so to conduct themselves that the negotiations are meaningful, which will not be the case when either of them insists upon its own position without contemplating any modification of it.

48. During the 1980s, the United States was concerned that a radar installation near the Soviet city of Krasnoyarsk might be a violation of the terms of the 1972 Anti-Ballistic Missile Treaty, which sharply limits the types and locations of modern defensive radar facilities. The United States repeatedly pressed the Soviet leadership on this point, expressing dissatisfaction with the partial explanations and denials emanating from Moscow. The United States insisted that the Soviets be much more forthcoming regarding the details of the operation of the installation, alleging that the Soviet failure to cooperate in resolving the controversy was itself a problem under the dispute-resolution provisions of the treaty. Eventually, the Soviet leadership acknowledged that the radar was inconsistent with the treaty and promised to dismantle it. George Bunn, "Soviets Admit ABM Violation," *Arms Control Today* 19 (Nov. 1989), p. 27.

49. Throughout the 1980s, the United States government expressed concern that a 1979 outbreak of anthrax in the Soviet city of Sverdlovsk might be due to an accident at a biological weapons facility there, operating in violation of the 1972 Biological Weapons Convention. The Soviet government denied the charge, but declined to provide sufficient information or explanation to put the concerns to rest. Again, the United States in that situation demanded punctilious adherence to the terms of the treaty, including the dispute resolution provisions, and upbraided the Soviets for failure to cooperate more fully in resolving the controversy. See Elisa Harris, "Sverdlovsk and Yellow Rain: Two Cases of Soviet Noncompliance?," 11 *International Security* No. 4 (Spring 1987), p. 41.

50. In the annual compliance report (where the administration advised the Congress about incidents related to Soviet adherence with arms control agreements), the United States complained that "[O]ur repeated attempts to discuss these occurrences with Soviet authorities have been rebuffed . . . Soviet refusal to discuss this matter calls into question their sincerity on the whole range of arms control agreements." Soviet Noncompliance With Arms Control Agreements, President's unclassified report, December 2, 1987, reprinted in *Department of State Bulletin* (Mar. 1988), pp. 51, 54.

51. Restatement, footnote no. 25, §336; John Rhinelander and George Bunn, "Who's Bound by the Former Soviet Union's Arms Control Treaties?," *Arms Control Today* 21 (Dec. 1991), p. 3.

52. Vienna Convention, footnote no. 25, Article 62.

53. This change of mind by the Reagan and Bush administrations about the obligations of the NPT is strikingly similar, at core, to the more notorious proposed "reinterpretation" of the Anti-Ballistic Missile Treaty. There, too, the executive branch attempted to depart from the long-held consensus understanding of the meaning of an important arms control agreement, and the Congress—and the other state party to the treaty—reacted vigorously. See symposium, "Arms Control Treaty Reinterpretation," 137 *Pennsylvania Law Review* No. 5 (1989).

54. Vienna Convention, footnote no. 25, Articles 60, 65 and 66.

55. Vienna Convention, footnote no. 25, Articles 60–62. Similar remedies are available to the innocent party aggrieved by the other party's breach of a bilateral agreement, such as the TTBT. Id. at 60.1.

56. Analogously, under the TTBT, Russia could assert the right to suspend or terminate the 150 kiloton ceiling or any of the verification procedures incorporated into the treaty and its protocols.

57. The TTBT provides parallel opportunities. The treaty has an initial five-year duration and is automatically extended for successive five year periods unless either party terminates it. The treaty also establishes a Joint Consultative Commission, where the parties may, *inter alia*, "consider questions concerning compliance with the obligations assumed." TTBT, footnote no. 12, Articles V.1(b) and VIII.1.

58. Experts have concluded that the 1995 conference would not be authorized to amend the treaty or to make its extension directly conditional upon the conclusion of another instrument such as a CTBT. Thomas Graham, Jr., "The Duration of the Nuclear Non-Proliferation Treaty: Sudden Death or New Lease on Life?," 29 *Virginia Journal of International Law* 661 (1989); George Bunn and Charles N. Van Doren, "Options for Extension of the NPT: The Intention of the Drafters of Article X.2," in George Bunn, David Fischer and Charles N. Van Doren, *Options and Opportunities: The NPT Extension Conference of 1995* (Programme for Promoting Nuclear Non-Proliferation, 1991); Bunn and Van Doren, "Two Options for the 1995 NPT Extension Conference Revisited," (Lawyers Alliance for World Security, Issue Brief, July 1992). A linkage in political, rather than legal terms, however, might be possible.

59. The formal procedure for amending the NPT is unusually cumbersome, requiring the affirmative support of a majority of parties, including all the NWS and all the states which are members of the IAEA Board of Governors. NPT, footnote no. 1, Article VIII.2.

60. The United States has withdrawn from the compulsory jurisdiction of the International Court of Justice, so there is little prospect of asserting effective jurisdiction in a contentious case testing compliance with Article VI. Organs of the United Nations do, however, retain the capacity to solicit an "advisory opinion" from the ICJ.

61. It is imaginable that the United States would attempt to rescue the situation before 1995 by proposing or concluding some additional international limitations upon nuclear testing, while once again stopping short of a full CTBT. Such an accord could, for example, limit the annual number of nuclear tests or reduce their maximum size from one hundred fifty kilotons to perhaps twenty-five or ten kilotons. It is, however, doubtful that any such interim accord would satisfy the more militant NNWS, unless it were linked to a fixed timetable ensuring its conversion into a permanent halt to all testing.

Publications List

Nuclear Non-Proliferation

6   *Two Options for the 1995 NPT Extension Conference Revisited,* by George Bunn and Charles N. Van Doren: Washington DC, (June 1992), $5.00 (photocopy).

7   *Who Inherited the Former Soviet Union's Obligations Under Arms Control Treaties with the United States?,* by George Bunn and John Rhinelander: Washington DC, (March 1992), $7.50.

8   *Nuclear Arms Contol: The U.S. and India,* A Report of the WCNP Study Group on U.S. Policy Option for Constraining Proliferation in South Asia: Washington DC, (May 1993), $5.00.

9   *Strengthening the NPT in the Post-Cold War World,* by James F. Leonard: WCNP Working Paper No. 1, Washington, DC, (October 1992), $5.00.

10   *The Changing Nature of Global Security and its Impact on South Asia,* Robert S. McNamara, Address to the Indian Defense Policy Forum, (November 20, 1992), $5.00.

11   *Disarming Iraq: Preparing for the Long-Term Monitoring of Iraq's Nuclear Weapons Capability,* discussion and debate featuring Ambassador Michael Newlin, former Deputy Executive Chairman of the UN Special Commission on Iraq, moderated by James Leonard: WCNP Briefing Report, Washington, DC (October 26, 1992), $5.00.

Chemical & Biological Weapons

12   *Some Disassembly Required: Eliminating Chemical Weapons While Protecting the Environment,* by David A. Koplow: Washington DC, (May 1994), $10.00.

13   *Public Trust and Technology: Chemical Weapons Destruction in the United States. Consequences of Crucial Technology Colliding with Unyielding Political Difficulties.* A Discussion with Dr. Mark Brown, Senior Analyst at the Office of Technology Assessment: Oceans and Environment: Washington DC, (December 1992), $7.50.

14 *Antichemical Protection and the Chemical Weapons Convention.* eds. Deshingkar, Priyamwanda, Matthew Meselson and Julian Perry Robinson, Harvard Sussex Program on CBW Armament and Arms Limitation: Washington DC, 1993, $15.00.

15 *Banning Non-Lethal Chemical Incapacitants in the Chemical Weapons Convention.* A Briefing Discussion with Dr. Matthew Meselson, Professor of Biochemistry at Harvard University: Washington DC, (1992), $5.00.

16 *A Status Report on the Chemical Weapons Convention Negotiations.* A Briefing Discussion with Brad Roberts, Editor of the *Washington Quarterly* and Expert on Chemical Weapons Control Issues: Washington DC, (1992), $3.00.

17 *The Lessons of Iraq: Unconventional Weapons, Inspection and Verification, and the United Nations and Disarmament.* A Briefing and Discussion with Johan Molander, Special Adviser to the Chairman, United Nations Special Commission on Iraq: Washington DC, (November 1991), $5.00.

18 *Control of Biological Weapons in the New World Order.* A Briefing and Discussion with Dr. Barbara Hatch Rosenberg: Washington DC, (October 1991), $5.00.

Use the form on page 112 to order these publications.

Publications Order Form

To order publications, please send a check or money order made payable to "LAWS/CNS", 1601 Connecticut Ave, NW, #600, Washington, DC 20009. tel. (202) 745-2450, fax (202) 667-0444.

O Enclosed is a check made payable to LAWS/CNS

O Charge my: O VISA   O MasterCard   O CarteBlanche

CARD NUMBER_____EXP. DATE_____

SIGNATURE_____

NAME/INSTITUTION_____

ADDRESS_____

CITY/STATE/ZIP/COUNTRY_____

Order #	Quantity	Price

* Bulk orders available at a special rate.
  Contact Heather Press, CNS, (202) 745-2450.

Total | $